Business Objects: Software Solutions

Business Objects: Software Solutions

Edited by

Kathy Spurr
Analysis Design Consultants, UK
Chairman, BCS CASE Specialist Group

Paul Layzell
UMIST, Manchester, UK

Leslie Jennison
TI Information Engineering UK Ltd, UK

Neil Richards
Neil Richards and Company, UK

JOHN WILEY & SONS
Chichester · New York · Brisbane · Toronto · Singapore

Copyright © 1994 by John Wiley & Sons Ltd,
Baffins Lane, Chichester,
West Sussex PO19 1UD, England

National (01243) 779777
International (+44) 1243 779777

Reprinted January 1995, June 1995

Other Wiley Editorial Offices

John Wiley & Sons, Inc., 605 Third Avenue,
New York, NY 10158–0012, USA

Jacaranda Wiley Ltd, 33 Park Road, Milton,
Queensland 4064, Australia

John Wiley & Sons (Canada) Ltd, 22 Worcester Road,
Rexdale, Ontario M9W 1L1, Canada

John Wiley & Sons (SEA) Pte Ltd, 37 Jalan Pemimpin #05-04,
Block B, Union Industrial Building, Singapore 2057

British Library Cataloguing in Publication Data

A catalogue record for this book is available from the British Library

ISBN 0 471 95187 0

Typeset in 10/12pt Palatino from author's disks by
Jeremy Thompson Publishing Services, Market Harborough
Printed and bound in Great Britain by
Biddles Ltd, Guildford and King's Lynn

Contents

Preface

When we build, let us think that we build for ever.
John Ruskin, 1819-1900

WHY ARE OBJECTS IMPORTANT?

The concept of an Object is recognised as an important innovation for software developers, offering the opportunity to improve productivity and reliability, and providing a more intuitive approach to application design. It is important, too, for business professionals, who can analyse the structure and workings of an enterprise through the creation of object oriented business models.

For those concerned with Business Re-Engineering, business objects can be used to identify essential business components, thereby providing a foundation for re-engineering activity, facilitating redesign of interfaces and messaging.

By using an appropriate software development platform, business objects can be implemented directly in code, providing savings in the overall development effort, through effective reuse, as well as a closer match between the business problem and the software solution.

AN INDUSTRIAL REVOLUTION IN SOFTWARE DEVELOPMENT

Software development is considered a 'high-technology' industry. But, until recently, software production techniques had been limited by the prevailing 'craft culture' philosophy, which refused to value a solution, unless it had been painstakingly hand-coded. This craft culture is reaching the end of its days, since it has proved ineffective in dealing with on-going changes to user requirements, and is too slow and rigid to keep pace with inevitable technology innovations. The object modelling paradigm, together with supporting tools, provides us with an enabling technology, which takes us to the verge of an industrial revolution in software production. We can now begin to make use of power tools and engineering methods, and so turn the vision of a software factory into reality.

WHAT IS AN OBJECT?

An object can be regarded as an instance which encapsulates data and process. It has hidden information, and defined public access. Objects send messages to other objects, thereby providing communication and system functionality.

Objects are grouped into classes, which may form part of an inheritance hierarchy, where sub-classes inherit all properties of the super-classes, unless these properties are specifically disallowed, or redefined. Inheritance and polymorphism provide important mechanisms for reuse, which is enabled through the use of class libraries. Using an appropriate development environment, object models can be implemented directly in code.

(A short tutorial on object modelling is provided following the introduction.)

WHAT IS OBJECT ORIENTED DEVELOPMENT?

Analysis is the process of obtaining and clarifying our understanding of the problem. Design involves the construction of a solution. It is important to recognise that a given problem may result in more than one satisfactory solution. The object oriented approach enables us to model the business problem immediately in terms of objects, which can map directly to design and implementation constructs, thereby shortening the traditional development life cycle.

Object oriented development encourages us to adopt a manufacturing philosophy which includes the creation of architectural business objects, specifically designed for reuse. We should recognise, therefore, that analysis activities are affected. Since reuse is inherent in the object paradigm, we are forced to investigate the applicability of architecture objects as part of our problem domain.

Since the object oriented approach avoids a transformation of the problem space, we are less likely to lose important problem details than when using more traditional approaches, which consider data and processes separately. When using object oriented techniques, proportionally more effort is devoted to analysis, rather than other phases of the life-cycle. Considerable emphasis is placed upon getting a clean analysis model, before implementation takes place. This forces the resulting system to be closely linked with the real-world problem, producing a more satisfactory model, especially when later changes in the real-world requirements require maintenance of the system.

BUSINESS OBJECTS AND SOFTWARE ARCHITECTURE

Business objects model fundamental business entities that recur across projects in a given domain. Examples would include a bank account, customer and a gas turbine. Well understood business abstractions can be reused across the application portfolio, reaping benefits in terms of increased productivity. Additionally, higher quality is achieved because such objects are the cornerstone of future business systems and therefore there is a strong motivation for greater investment in their development to ensure quality, reliability and efficiency.

A business can leverage benefit through the use of a software architecture or framework: a higher level abstraction that captures business objects together with their interactions, providing ready made solutions to a wide range of business problems.

Although simple in principle, encapsulating the right information in the right objects with the right relationships is a considerable challenge, requiring an analytical approach, combined with an awareness of the aesthetics of good design.

WHO SHOULD READ THIS BOOK?

This book is of interest to:

- IT managers and consultants concerned with gaining maximum competitive advantage through the use of object models
- IT practitioners who wish to use object oriented techniques to support their own design and development work
- Professionals of any discipline who may wish to use object oriented analysis to model their business problems
- Developers and vendors of object oriented software development tools, who need to understand the requirements and evolution of this growing market

- Industrial or Commercial organisations looking to adopt object technology or object oriented CASE products
- Lecturers and students in business and computer studies who wish to understand the interplay of business need, object oriented techniques and tools in this key field of study.

WHAT DOES THIS BOOK CONTAIN?

This book is based on papers contributed to two seminars, held in London in July and Manchester in September 1994. The seminars were accompanied by an exhibition of tools, details of which appear in this book.

This book reflects the thoughts and experience of those concerned with object oriented development. Some are independent consultants, others represent some of the leading providers of object oriented development tools. They can guide us to some stimulating ideas and research, and help us to prepare for exploiting object technology in our own work.

THE BRITISH COMPUTER SOCIETY CASE GROUP

The seminar was organised by the British Computer Society CASE specialist group, formed in 1989, as an independent, non-partisan forum for debate on CASE and related issues. The group believe that this is an appropriate time to hold this seminar, because object oriented analysis and design tools are emerging, and organisations now are seeking to gain maximum competitive advantage through the use of such tools.

This is the fifth book which has been published on behalf of the BCS CASE specialist group by John Wiley and Sons. The first two volumes, *CASE on Trial* (1990) and *CASE: Current Practice, Future Prospects* (1992) dealt directly with Computer Assistance for Software Engineering.

The next two books broadened the scope of CASE to incorporate Computer Assistance for the wider activity of Systems Engineering. *Software Assistance for Business Re-Engineering* (1993) continued the theme of computer support, but was directed more towards analytical techniques for understanding the business rather than direct production of a software solution. *Computer Support for Co-operative Work* (1994) focused on software assistance for group working. It is not a necessary prerequisite for the current book to have read the previous four volumes.

THANK YOU

The editors would like to thank those authors who submitted papers for the seminar. In all cases, the contributors had to work to very tight deadlines, in order to meet the publication date. Thanks also to the production staff at John Wiley and Sons for their patience and tolerance, and for unending good humour when the late delivery of contributions continually threatens to throw their production process into disarray.

Kathy Spurr
Paul Layzell
Leslie Jennison
Neil Richards
July 1994

Authors' Addresses

EDITORS

Kathy Spurr

Analysis Design Consultants
Lyndhurst Lodge
41 Lyndhurst Road
Chichester
West Sussex
PO19 2LE

Paul Layzell

Department of Computation
UMIST
PO Box 88
Manchester
M60 1QD

Leslie Jennison

Frogmore House
Market Place
Box
Corsham
Wilts
SN14 9NZ

Neil Richards

Neil Richards and Company
Hobbits
Danesbury Park Road
Welwyn
Herts
AL6 9SS

AUTHORS

Tim Boreham

Nutat Technologies
116 Albert Street, Suite 812
Ottawa, Ontario
Canada
K1S 3P7

Philip Carnelly

Ovum Limited
1 Mortimer Street
London
W1N 7RH

John Dodd

TI Information Engineering Limited
James Martin House
Littleton Road
Ashford
Middx
TW15 1TZ

Stuart Frost

SELECT Software Tools Ltd
Idsall House
High Street
Prestbury
Cheltenham
Gloucs
GL52 3AY

Don Kavanagh

Interactive Development Environments Ltd
28 Darely Road
Burbage
Hinckley
Leics
LE10 2RL

Allan S. Kennedy,
Adrian F. King and
Ian T. Wilkie

Kennedy Carter
1 Thornton Road
London
SW19 4NB

Eric Leach

Eric Leach Marketing Ltd
2 Bell Road
Hounslow
TW3 3NN

Gemma R. Overboom

Koninklijke/ Shell Exploratie en
Prodiktie Laboratorium
P.O. Box 60, 2280 AB Rijswijk
The Netherlands

Howard Ricketts

Softcase Consulting Limited
The Loft
13 Ravine Road
Canford Cliffs
Poole
BH13 7HS

Nick Whitehead

Cadre Technologies Ltd
Centennial Court
East Hampstead Road
Bracknell
RG12 1JA

Trademarks

Motif is a trademark of The Open Software Foundation Incorporated

ObjectIQ is a trademark of Hitachi

ObjectStore, ObjectTeam and Teamwork are registered trademarks of Cadre Technologies Inc.

ObjectWorks, Smalltalk, ParcPlace Smalltalk and Smalltalk-80 are trademarks of ParcPlace Systems Inc.

ONTOS is a trademark of ONTOS Inc.

OpenWindows, Solaris, SPARC, SparcWorks, Sun, SunOS are trademarks of Sun Microsystems Incorporated.

Oracle is a registered trademark of Oracle corporation

Powerbuilder is a trademark of Powersoft Corporation

Prokappa is a trademark of Intellicorp Inc.

Raima is a trademark of Raima Corporation

Rational and Rational Rose are trademarks of Rational

SmallTalk and Visual SmallTalk are trademarks of Digitalk Inc.

SNAP is a trademark of Template Software

Software through Pictures and IDE are trademarks of IDE (Interactive Development Environments) Inc.

Sybase is a trademark of Sybase Inc.

TEXEL and VSF are copyright of Virtual Software Factory Limited

Toolbuilder is a trademark of Ipsys Software plc

Uniface is a trademark of Natural Language Systems Inc.

UNIX is a trademark of UNIX System Laboratories Inc.

Versant is a trademark of Versant Object Technology

X Window System is a trademark of the Massachusetts Institute of Technology.

Introduction

Kathy Spurr, Paul Layzell, Leslie Jennison

ABSTRACT

This paper discusses the use of object models for both business and software engineering. Software tool support for object modelling is discussed in terms of its current and potential capabilities. The changing role of the software practitioner is addressed, moving from that of a software engineer to a software systems architect. It is recognised that business objects will have an important role in future software development activities. This paper also serves as an introduction to the other chapters in the book.

WHY OBJECT ORIENTED?

Mainstream computing has a history of some 40–50 years. In that time, the nature of the tasks carried out by a software professional has changed dramatically. Early software development focused on painstaking, labour intensive production of accurate and efficient procedural code. This code was represented initially in the form of primitive machine instructions, before the use of more accessible assembler; then eventually in the form of rich, sophisticated languages, such as COBOL, Fortran, Pascal and C.

With such languages, developers used top-down analysis and fragmentation techniques to simplify the problem. They advocated partitioning of processes, and the separation of data from procedural aspects. For many years, systems were designed successfully using this paradigm, and a body of effective CASE tools was developed to provide computer assistance for the construction of analysis models and the automatic generation of code. In this respect, component CASE (C-CASE) and

Integrated CASE (I-CASE) represent extremes of a spectrum of tools which provide computer support. Component CASE allows an analyst to produce discrete models which have little or no integrity checking or synchronisation. Integrated CASE allows analysts to produce totally consistent, synchronised models, with integrity checks enforced at source. Currently, many good CASE tools exist, running on a range of development platforms, and in a range of price bands, each providing a different level of support for integration along this spectrum.

As CASE tools have evolved, a new vision of software development has emerged. Traditional development approaches (which separated data from procedure) suffered from an inability to deal with ongoing change. Software designs which had been based on procedures did not respond well to changes in requirements. Even a small change in requirements could have dramatic and far reaching effects on the overall system. This caused unmanageable backlogs in change requests, some of which became too impractical to implement at all. Problems arose because the software model grew out of sync. with the real world that it was supposed to reflect.

In addition, the total volume of software has been increasing, and many practitioners have felt the frustration of being unable to reuse existing code, or having to rewrite software from scratch, which is identical, or similar to existing code.

Object oriented techniques are a response to these difficulties. Having its origin in programming languages such as Simula and Smalltalk, the object oriented paradigm provides effective mechanisms for software reuse, and enables the software solution to be bound tightly to the business problem, thus providing software which is more resilient to change, and also an effective mechanism for modelling, and re-engineering the business.

WHAT IS OBJECT ORIENTED?

A short tutorial on object oriented philosophy and terminology is provided in the tutorial following this introduction, for the benefit of those readers who are unfamiliar with the paradigm. We use an example of a simple order processing system. This does not imply that object oriented techniques can only be applied to 'data processing' type applications. On the contrary, object modelling can be used very successfully on a wide variety of projects. The editors have used object modelling for telecommunications systems, graphical user interface design, distributed processing, client-server systems, CASE tool prototyping, and real-time applications. Other contributors have chosen examples which reflect their own special experiences in this area. We choose a simple example deliberately, which we hope all readers will understand.

Readers who are unfamiliar with the object oriented paradigm should review the tutorial at this point.

BUSINESS OBJECTS AND REUSE

In recent years, object technology has shown benefits in key areas. Objects are essential concepts in graphical user interface design, and a rich variety of development environments and class libraries is emerging.

Inheritance and Polymorphism are crucial to the successful re-use of class definitions, and the role played by the class library in this respect is important. In graphical user interface design, for example, frequently used classes such as scroll bars, listboxes, windows and buttons are readily available at the click of a mouse button.

This concept is being extended to other application areas. In the telecommunications field, for example, standard classes have been specially developed in C++ which are available for purchase. We predict that the specialist class library will become a new growth commodity.

Our tutorial example, the retail warehouse order system, contains a group of classes which could easily form part of a class library prepared for a specialist business application. In fact, the classes order, customer, stock item occur in all order processing systems. In essence, one order processing system is much like another. There would be clear benefits in providing standard classes such as this within the development environment. Business professionals have no difficulty with comprehending the objects they use within their own environment. We will call these 'Business Objects' (as opposed to technology driven objects such as list boxes, buttons, windows and scroll bars).

A business professional would readily understand the meaning of the classes 'order', 'stock item' and 'customer', since these are concepts extracted directly from their environment. There may be a little difficulty with comprehending the somewhat artificial construct 'order line item', but this need not be a problem, since it can be hidden within the higher level object 'order' which is understood.

We can extend this concept of 'business object' to an even higher level of abstraction. A software development company of our acquaintance recently produced one such large object, which was utilised successfully. The object in question was sold to two other companies, reused, adapted and utilised to take account of the particular characteristics of the new corporations.

This business object was a complete 'frequent flier system', familiar to the majority of air travellers.

SOFTWARE DEVELOPMENT: ARCHITECTURE NOT ENGINEERING

We see object technology providing an important shift in our design practice. The use of CASE tools and object technology provide us with mechanisms so that we can move away from the inefficiencies and dissatisfaction inherent in the dubious craft industry of low level software production.

In the normal everyday world, the term 'craft' industry' has a certain magical rural charm, conjuring up visions of old world quality. This has not been our experience in software development, at the low level of hand-coding. We cannot afford the luxury of hand-crafting our code from scratch every time we wish to create or maintain a software system. When implemented on a large scale, and without inspired leadership, such practices produce code of dubious long-term quality, and can be accompanied by frustration and dissatisfaction on the part of developers.

Therefore, we feel that the future lies with careful automation of the software development process, accompanied by good architectures and frameworks. To exploit fully both CASE and object technology, we need effective class libraries which will encourage us actively to reuse and exploit business object definitions at varying levels of abstraction

In this sense, we view the user of an object oriented CASE tool as somewhat akin to the Architect who uses a CAD (Computer Aided Design) package. Architects require standard libraries of measured components (such as doors, windows, basins, etc.). A good CAD package will have the facility to import libraries, which have been purchased separately. Library components are selected by pointing and clicking with the mouse, so that these may be effortlessly incorporated into the design.

The emphasis is on standard measurements and definitions, so that, when building, components may easily be purchased off the shelf. For architects, these libraries are readily available on CD-ROM.

We would like to encourage a similar approach to software design. We hope that object oriented CASE vendors will incorporate mechanisms for importing and exporting class definitions as required. We look forward to a time when reliable, standard, tested class libraries containing business specific objects are freely available as a purchased commodity.

We hope that object technology can free software practitioners from the chains of technology-driven development, so that they can concentrate their efforts on the production of software which has vision and creativity, and responds flexibly to the changing needs of the business. We see the evolving role of the software practitioner as more akin to that of an architect, rather than an engineer.

THE PAPERS IN THIS BOOK

The aim of this book is to provide insight into the role of CASE technology in object oriented development. For convenience the papers appear in three sections, each of which addresses a key theme.

Section 1: Business Objects and Software Architectures for Effective Re-Use
The first theme focuses upon the issue of reuse. One of the most common justifications for the move to object technology is the potential for reuse. Whilst the basic components are in place for reuse (such as class libraries, information hiding, inheritance and polymorphism), the object oriented approach has, until now, lacked an organisational capability. Without this, there is little or no direction in terms of which components should be reused nor how they should be managed.

The response to this problem of scaling up to industrial level reuse has seen the emergence of software architectures, business objects and a component-based approach to software construction. The papers in Section 1 therefore focus upon these broad issues of reuse, components and frameworks.

John Dodd begins with a basic exposition on the use of business objects as the most relevant software components within an information system. He outlines the two main tasks within a manufacturing culture: component manufacture and component assembly. This provides an overall management framework, as well as requirements for CASE tool support. Stuart Frost's paper extends this framework by developing some of the more detailed issues within the object life-cycle, particularly by introducing the notion of incremental development.

Allan Kennedy and his co-authors begin with a brief examination of the problems with existing models of development and their supporting tools, bringing out the advantages of domain analysis and software architectures for more effective development. The paper ends with a set of requirements for future object oriented CASE tools and a review of a particular object oriented analysis tool.

Finally, Tim Boreham's paper addresses the issue of reuse in object oriented analysis. Through practical application, he has developed an approach to reuse at a level above conventional source code, in which basic building blocks are identified and used to construct system fragments.

Section 2: Development Methods and Tools
Having discussed the broad issues of reuse and development frameworks, the papers in Section 2 address the issue of techniques, methods and tools for object oriented development. To date a large variety of object oriented methods have been published in the literature and these are being applied increasingly to commercial system development. But, as experience is gained, there is a noticeable trend towards the consolidation and integration of techniques as happened with structured methods in the 1970s and 1980s. Section 2 therefore looks at some developments within the object oriented methods arena, ending with an analysis of CASE tool support for these emerging 'supermethods'.

Section 2 opens with Don Kavanagh's paper, in which he reviews James Rumbaugh's OMT method, together with two extensions identified as bringing particular benefit to the requirements elicitation process. These extensions are Rebecca Wirfs-Brock's CRC (Class Responsibility Collaboration) technique and Ivor Jacobson's 'Use Case' approach. Howard Ricketts' paper describes a different synthesis of techniques which has led to the development of Hewlett Packard's Fusion method. In both cases, the authors identify specific requirements of CASE technology support and in the Ricketts paper, describe a CASE tool for supporting Fusion (product details are included in Section 4)

However much techniques and methods are integrated, application developers will always be confronted with a wide ranging toolkit. Gemma Overboom's paper is therefore helpful in presenting two case studies concerning the selection of object oriented techniques where seven methods were evaluated, leading to the selection of OMT.

As with all techniques and methods, CASE technology provides the ability to deliver effective system solutions within a controlled and manageable framework. Philip Carnelley presents a useful paper which reviews tool support for object oriented development methods—reflecting on the past and looking forwards to the future.

Section3: Managing the Transition
Now attention turns to the more pragmatic issues of managing object oriented development, particularly addressing issues such as the move to object oriented technology from more conventional software development approaches, as well as the important issue of supporting technology standards.

Nick Whitehead's paper takes a management oriented perspective, looking at the more general issues of method transition. Eric Leach's paper ends Section 3 by reviewing the impact of object oriented technology together with some of the impending standardisation issues and definitions which are beginning to emerge. In particular, he looks at the Object Management Group's (OMG) 'Object Model', and their standards agenda for the next few years.

Section 4: Selected Software Tools
Finally, in Section 4 the book details some software for supporting object oriented development.

EXPLOITING OBJECT TECHNOLOGY

Those who wish to reap the benefits of object technology in their business might begin by reflecting on the way that information technologies have recently evolved and the lessons that can be learnt about their implementation.

The evolution of object technology began with programming environments and the re-use of technical objects, especially in the design of graphical user interface software. Interest in extending the exploitation of objects to other stages in the development life-cycle has moved up the architectural layers from technology to design, then to requirements analysis, and now, at length to strategies and architectures. In this respect, the evolution of object technology parallels and extends the emergence of a rich variety of techniques from database and data sharing technology to populate 'structured methods' development and underpin today's industrial strength CASE tools.

In the information systems development field we have learned a lot about how the use of CASE interacts with methods and techniques to evolve more iterative life-cycles, to reuse analysis and design components, and to apply more rigour to system definition. Consultants and users of CASE have discovered that implementing a new technology involves process and organisational change that cannot be done overnight. CASE technology has to support group working and concurrent development, and previous investment in (legacy) systems and data cannot be ignored.

Early applications development which used object oriented analysis and design techniques (such as those described in Booch, 1986) occurred in real time control systems. Many of those developers were influenced by an engineering culture with a growing tradition of reuse and evolving design components. This was driven by pressures on cost and development time in defence and aerospace industries that are mirrored by today's business drivers of process re-engineering (Spurr *et al.*, 1993). To some, it seems natural, therefore to integrate into application development the disciplines of architecture management (previously attempted with mixed success in isolation in Integrated Project Support Environments—IPSEs), and those of concurrent engineering, and design of classes or components for reuse.

Revolution or evolution?

Many of the papers in this book demonstrate an awareness of the inter-relationships of these threads. There are however some in the object market place who cry that object technology in isolation is the answer to all shortcomings; that it alone will revolutionise the development process if we remake all objects anew. There are also the vendors and early adopters of point solution object technology tools who claim that success in some small or isolated projects supports this viewpoint. Previous experience of introducing new approaches into an organisation tells us that we cannot ignore the existing development process and operational systems and simply start afresh.

Perhaps, fortunately, not all is as new as it seems. An object can be a simpler thing for a business to understand, but method and tool support for the more complex underlying concepts of data, activity and control have been well tried in structured methods and CASE technology. Some of the classic expositions of object design are provided by former proponents of structured methods (Coad and Yourdon, 1991; Martin and Odell, 1993; Shlaer and Mellor, 1988). Some of the papers in this book display a vision of how object technologies and other techniques can co-exist as part of an evolving process.

We may learn better from trials of this new technology if we remember also how long it took to reach a mature assessment of similar early claims for CASE tools and structured methods. We may be alarmed that some tool builders seem likely to endure a period of expensively re-inventing the infrastructure of so-called 'conventional' CASE tools, but we should also be encouraged to see other object oriented tool providers addressing the issues of requirements management, reuse management, group working, and interworking with existing applications. None of this should prevent us from trying and learning from some of the reasonably priced tools now becoming available in increasing numbers.

CONCLUSION

As we have recently pointed out against the background of co-operative working environments (Spurr *et al.*, 1994), we cannot expect to implement new technologies in isolation. In this book, several papers and tools address implementation issues in the context of other technologies such as client-server. There is also a general growth in understanding that we must manage the development process, taking account of business needs. In this spirit we encourage you to understand the business as well as the technical implications of the coming explosion of tool support for the exciting possibilities of object oriented development.

REFERENCES

Booch G. 1986. Object Oriented Development. *IEEE Transactions on Software Engineering* **12**; 211-221.

Coad P. and Yourdon E. 1991a. *Object Oriented Analysis.* Yourdon Computing Press.

Coad P and Yourdon E. 1991b. *Object Oriented Design.* Yourdon Computing Press.

Martin J and Odell J. 1992. *object-oriented Analysis and Design.* Prentice Hall.

Rumbaugh J, Blaha M, Premerlani W, Eddy F and Lorensen W. 1991. *Object-Oriented Modeling and Design.* Prentice Hall.

Shlaer S and Mellor S. 1988. *Object-Oriented Systems Analysis: Modeling the World in Data.* Yourdon Press.

Spurr K, Layzell P, Jennison L and Richards N. 1993. *Software Assistance for Business Re-Engineering.* Wiley.

Spurr K, Layzell P, Jennison, L and Richards N. 1994. *Computer Support for Co-Operative Work.* Wiley.

What are Business Objects? A Brief Tutorial

Kathy Spurr

ABSTRACT

A short tutorial on object oriented philosophy and terminology is provided, for the benefit of those readers who are unfamiliar with the paradigm. We choose a simple example of an order processing system containing business objects, which we hope all readers will understand. This system is described using features of the OMT notation developed by Rumbaugh *et al.* (1991).

By this simple example, we do not imply that object oriented techniques are only suitable for 'data processing' type applications. We recognise that object technology is suitable for a wide range of application environments, including telecommunications, graphical user-interface design, distributed processing, real-time systems and event driven systems.

THE SAMPLE APPLICATION: A RETAIL WAREHOUSE ORDER SYSTEM

In a retail warehouse, a customer can place an order for one or more stock items. The name, address, telephone number and current debit balance are recorded for each customer. For each stock item, details are held of the description, unit cost, reorder level, quantity in stock and reorder quantity.

When a customer places an order for goods, they must provide their customer identification number, together with the stock reference numbers and quantity ordered for each stock item. The system will create an order, an example of which is shown in Figure 1. The retail warehouse has two types of customer; cash and account. An account customer has an account

Order Number: O1234 Customer Id: C1234 Name: J Smith		Address: 10 Downing Street, London Telephone: (071) 571 1212	
Description of Stock Item	**Quantity ordered**	**Unit Cost**	**Total Cost**
CD-ROM PowerMac	3 4	200 2000	600 8000
Total Cost of Order			8600

Figure 1   Sample Order Form

reference in addition to other attributes, and pays for their stock items by quoting this account reference.

OBJECT

An object represents an instance of some thing which is relevant to the problem. Examples of objects are shown in Figure 2.

We assume that each object can be identified uniquely, by an object-identifier, and that each object knows the class to which it belongs.

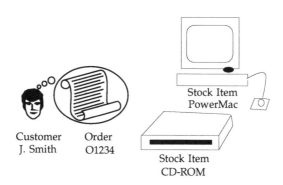

Customer   Order
J. Smith   O1234

Stock Item
PowerMac

Stock Item
CD-ROM

Figure 2   Examples of Business Objects in the Warehouse Order System

CLASS

A class represents a grouping of objects with properties in common. Classes in the warehouse ordering system are:

- Customer
- Order
- Stock Item

Objects which belong to each class will have the same types of attributes and operations as the other objects in that class. For example, we would expect all instances of the class 'Customer' to have a name, address, telephone number, and debit balance. All customers can change their address and pay their bills.

Using a notation similar to OMT (Rumbaugh *et al.*, 1991), we represent an object and a class as in Figure 3. Usually, analysis is done at the class level. Object diagrams are rarely drawn.

It is assumed that each object has an object-identifier, with which the object can uniquely be determined. Conventionally, we do not show these on the analysis model. In fact, it would be unwise to show these specifically as attributes during analysis, in case this constrained later design

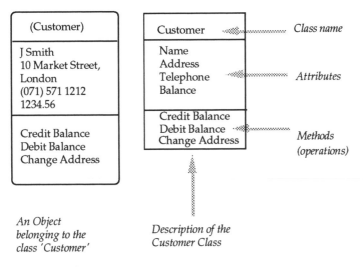

Figure 3   Example of Object Modelling Notation

decisions. (Object identifiers can be represented in the form of primary key attributes, integers or pointers depending on the chosen implementation environment.)

ASSOCIATIONS AND OPERATIONS

An association can be defined between two objects. The association is usually shown on a class diagram. Figure 4 shows an association 'places' between 'Customer' and 'Order', in the retail warehouse, indicating that

- Each customer places many orders (zero or more).
- Each order is placed by exactly one customer.

The association 'lists' between 'Order 'and 'Stock Item' shows that:

- Each order lists many stock items (one or more).
- Each stock item is listed on many orders (zero or more).

In such a model, we use two sentences to describe each association; one for the active tense of the verb, and the other for the passive tense. We adopt the convention that associations are read clockwise (so that, for example, customers place orders, rather than orders placing customers).

Each object has certain operations (methods, procedures) which it can perform or suffer. For example, a stock item object may be placed on order (presumably when the quantity in stock falls below the reorder level), or it may be issued.

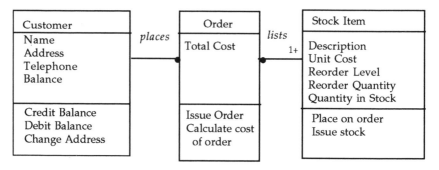

Figure 4   Examples of Associations

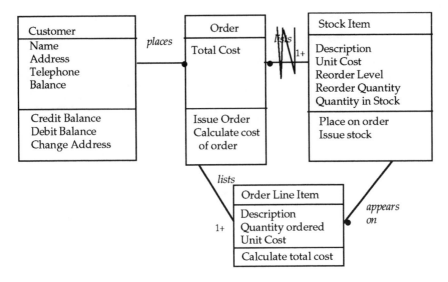

Figure 5 Resolving a Many: Many Association

RESOLVING MANY:MANY ASSOCIATIONS

The presence of a many: many association (such as 'lists' in Figure 4) gives us some cause for concern. Such an association may hide important details about the problem, and would be difficult to implement. We can simplify this association by introducing a new class 'order line item', as in Figure 5, enabling us to capture important information regarding the quantity of each stock item which has been ordered, and the cost. Having done this, we can remove the association 'lists' between 'Order' and 'Stock Item'.

AGGREGATION ASSOCIATIONS

In circumstances where one object forms part of another, we can make use of a special association: aggregation or assembly. Figure 6 demonstrates that an order may be treated as a collection of order line items.

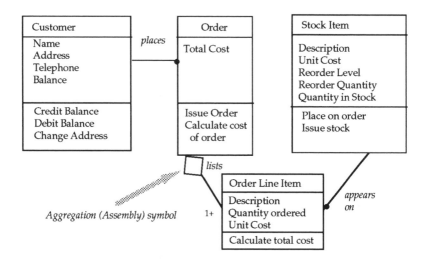

Figure 6   Order as a collection of Order Lines

INHERITANCE ASSOCIATIONS AND POLYMORPHISM

Inheritance and polymorphism are important considerations, since they provide essential reuse mechanisms. In this example, we know that there are two types of customer; cash and account. This enables us to define a class 'customer', as before, and to allow 'cash customer 'and 'account customer' to inherit properties from this super-class customer. Inheritance is shown in Figure 7.

A cash customer will inherit all properties from the parent class 'Customer', including the operation 'PayBill'. An account customer adapts and reuses the operation PayBill, but still preserves the same name for the operation. We say that the operation PayBill is 'overridden', since its implementation depends on the class in question. A cash customer will pay for their goods in the usual way, that is, using a cash payment. An account customer will pay for their goods by quoting an account reference. This leads us to an important feature of the object oriented paradigm—polymorphism. An operation will be polymorphic if it can take on different forms in different classes. The implementation of the operation depends on the context of its use.

A classic example of polymorphism in action concerns the operation 'Print'. We use the same command to print out many different types of file. Depending on the type of file, the operation will be implemented in

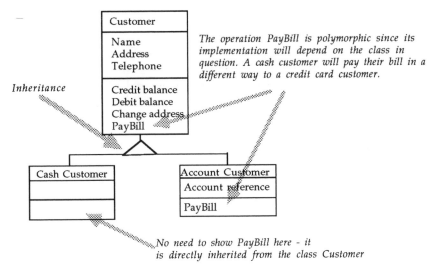

Figure 7   Inheritance and Polymorphism

many different ways. During analysis, we need not concern ourselves with this variety of implementation mechanisms.

STATES OF OBJECTS

Each object may exist in a number of different states. For example a stock item may be 'In stock', 'On order' (when the quantity in stock falls below the re-order level), or 'Out of stock'. These three states can be shown on a state diagram as in Figure 8.

The event 'Quantity in stock falls below zero' causes the stock item to change its state from being 'In stock' to being 'Out of stock'. This event also initiates the operation 'Issue out of stock message'.

MESSAGES

Objects communicate by sending messages to each other. Each object is assumed to exist in one of several states. We assume that objects can exist concurrently with other objects. Figure 9 shows an event trace when a customer places an order for stock items. Messages are used to notify objects of the occurrence of an event.

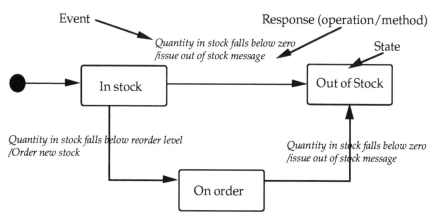

Figure 8   State Diagram for Stock Item

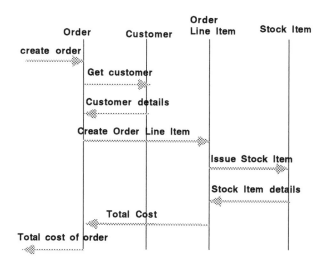

Figure 9   Event Traces when a Customer places an Order

REFERENCES

Rumbaugh J, Blaha M, Premerlani W, Eddy F and Lorensen W. 1991. *Object-Oriented Modelling and Design*. Prentice Hall.

Section 1

Business Objects and Software Architectures for Effective Reuse

1

Developing Information Systems from Components: the Role of CASE

John Dodd

ABSTRACT

The benefits of building applications from software components are described and business objects are advocated to be the most relevant software components for information systems. A component-based development approach is outlined. This involves two separate, but interacting development streams: one stream concentrates on component fabrication, the other on assembling an application. The fabrication of robust components which implement core business rules and policies, and which maintain data integrity, will continue to require professional IS developers. It will then be possible for department specialists and end-users to use these components to assemble their own applications, which they can use and incrementally improve in the production environment. The required CASE tool support is discussed, and the pivotal role played by the repository is explained. Finally, the possibilities for using today's CASE products for component-based development are explored.

Business Objects: Software Solutions. Edited by Kathy Spurr, Paul Layzell, Leslie Jennison
and Neil Richards
© 1994 John Wiley & Sons Ltd

THE NEW DEVELOPMENT APPROACH

In most corporations, the central IS[1] organisation faces some enormous challenges. Now that end-users have powerful, customisable office automation tools on their desks, there is an expectation that information systems should be able to offer the same levels of flexibility. Business process re-engineering has captured the enthusiasm of the managing director, and new, task-oriented, graphical applications are demanded— applications that enable employees to take responsibility for a business process from start to finish. Flatter management structures are the order of the day, and this requires employees to be empowered to access a wide range of company information and have the tools that aid decision making. User-departments are now building their own applications using low-cost PC software and database servers—to get round the backlog of central IS development. But these applications sometimes offer weak security, lack maintainability and discourage reuse and data integration. The business climate is changing continuously. Computer-technology must be used to enable that change, not just chase along afterwards.

We believe that companies can respond to these pressures by re-engineering the application development process. A shift to a component-based, *build-assemble-customise* pattern of development is advocated. A component-based approach offers new insights into how we might divide the tasks of application development among the groups of workers which have an interest.

Components intended for enterprise-wide use are a natural candidate for central development. Central developers would also take responsibility for assembling any applications which are to be used throughout the company. In addition, the central IS function would provide the technical infrastructure and application development advice to the rest of the company.

Components which implement the business rules of a particular department, or which are department-specific specialisations of enterprise-wide components, might now be built by domain specialists. Depending on the company's preference, the domain specialists could be located centrally or could reside within a departmental IS group. Domain specialists would also be expected to take the lead in assembling departmental applications. The departmental IS groups would, in any case, work in close harmony with central IS groups, sharing a common

---

[1]The term *central IS* will be used to when referring to the information systems development and maintenance organisation within an enterprise.

approach and common tools.

End-users would enjoy the ability to customise their applications—particularly the user interface. However, as businesses increasingly adopt the empowered worker model (in which users work within self-managed teams that have a cross-functional viewpoint), the ability for users—perhaps the more expert users—to assemble their own applications from existing components will enable them to fulfil their need to react rapidly to changes in their business. It is particularly this capacity to enable rapid response to change that suggests a component-based approach should be widely adopted as the next step in the evolution of application development.

Figure 1 illustrates how the work of building components, application assembly and application customisation might be distributed between the end-user, domain specialist and central specialist.

Build-assemble-customise is, then, a new development culture permitting department specialists to build and improve their own applications. Data sharing and software re-use are enabled through the use of software components. This paper introduces some of the elements of the new culture. It is arranged in three sections followed by a conclusion.

The first section explains the benefits of *software components* and proposes that business objects are the most relevant components within information systems. The following section describes a process for *component-based development*. This involves two separate, but interacting development streams: one stream concentrates on component fabrication, the other stream concentrates on assembling an application. The last section discusses the *role of CASE tools* within this development approach.

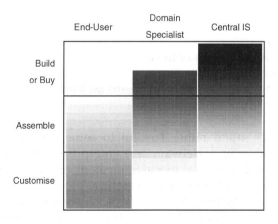

Figure 1   The New Development Pattern

Today's object-oriented and non-object-oriented CASE tools can be used. In the longer-term, a common repository that supports a variety of CASE tools is the best solution. This includes tools to build components and extract them from existing systems; tools that enable specialist staff to build large-scale information systems; and tools that allow end-users to iteratively develop ad hoc applications from their desktop.

SOFTWARE COMPONENTS

The Benefits of Components

Components are standard software parts, which can be assembled into larger parts and into applications. The manufacturing revolution occurred when goods started to be built from standard, interchangeable parts. The computer hardware industry has been outstandingly successful by assembling computers from standard integrated circuits and boards. Brad Cox (1990) argues the same can be done with software. Software production can be changed from a predominantly hand-crafted process into a less skilled assembly process, that is ideally performed by the consumers of the software themselves. Cox refers to this as the software industrial revolution.

The advantages of software components are seen to be:

- reliability: components that have been used in many applications are naturally well tried and tested
- reduced cost: if the components are used many times, development costs are shared
- reduced cycle times: applications are simply assembled from standard parts
- ease of change: it is easier to swap in new parts than it is to extend or correct monolithic software
- outsourcing: a market in components will emerge giving the option to build or buy.

While this may sound rather fanciful to some, we perceive that this movement is already underway, and enterprises need to decide now whether they wish to be one of the innovators, or whether they can risk waiting for component technology to mature.

The object concept has proved to be a very successful basis for standard software components. An object is a software unit that simulates a real-world object. An object remembers its state (data values) and contains operations to manipulate and report its state. The object hides all its details, and only exposes its operation interfaces to its users (see Figure 2). So the internal implementation of the object need not be known by its users, and can be upgraded without major repercussions within an application. The object concept has been successfully applied in many domains, but especially in engineering applications, software products and graphical user interface tools. Wilkie (1993) and Booch (1994) give examples.

Business Objects as Components

This paper proposes that *business objects* are the most useful kind of object for information system builders. A business object is a software unit that corresponds to a real world entity from the user's domain. In the words of Shelton, "business objects are abstractions about some real world person, place or thing. Business object examples include: product, customer, vendor, shipment, vehicle, circuit and employee" (Shelton, 1993). A business object is an entity (as in entity modelling) *and* its processes. Just as entity occurrences are classified into entity types, it is useful to classify business objects by business object type. Analysts and designers will concentrate on identifying, defining and constructing business object types, whose data definitions and processes then apply to all run-time instances of that business object type.

Business object types are relatively stable, and readily recognisable by business personnel. Compared with re-usable modules, business object

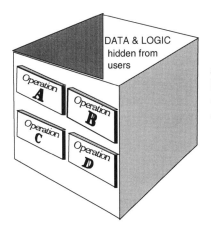

An object is a software "black box" which:
- offers *operations* to users
- encapsulates its *state* and *methods*

Figure 2   The concept of an Object

types should be easy for developers and users to locate and understand. A business object type bundles together all the attributes of an entity type and the standard processes that apply to the entity type in one logical package. An individual business object will remember the data about itself by storing its attribute values in a database while it is not in use. In the jargon of object-orientation, we propose that business objects are always persistent.

Business object types protect the integrity of shared data, and make it accessible in a standard way to all business personnel that need it. Business object types offer standard business calculations, and apply standard business policies in the form of *operations*. For each operation, its input parameters, return values and purpose are published. While some business object types may be enterprise-wide, others may be local to departments or small groups of users. The important thing is they are easily and safely shared by everyone who needs to use them.

Today, many business rules and calculations are already defined in software—but they are locked into traditionally designed, monolithic applications or hidden in personal spreadsheets and the like. It may be possible to extract operations from traditional applications, but the rules built into personal spreadsheets are generally uncontrolled, unknown and not re-usable.

Business objects differ from the object types typically available in today's OO language class libraries. These are generally technical objects, such as data types, DBMS interfaces and GUI components, which have to be requested from within object-oriented programming languages. (Shelton terms them foundation objects.) These are not real-world objects as far as business personnel are concerned, and it is the role of CASE tools to hide these technical objects from application builders. Foundation objects have enabled programmers to build impressive applications, as well as software products such as CASE tools. But—it is business objects that the new breed of non-technical application builder needs on his or her desk top, and foundation objects should be hidden beneath the covers are far as possible[2].

COMPONENT-BASED DEVELOPMENT

Twin Track Development

The component-based development approach involves two separate, but

---

[2]Ideally, a CASE tool should allow the more technical developer to add new or specialise existing GUI components, data types and data management objects, which can then be utilised by non-technical application builders.

interacting, development streams which address different objectives:

- the Component Fabrication Stream delivers re-usable business object servers;
- the Application Assembly Stream delivers automated support for business processes.

Figure 3 summarises the deliverables, rationale and major development tasks of each stream. *Business object servers* are the executable modules which bundle together one or several business object operations.

Business object operations perform application-independent checks and calculations, applying business policies and rules. Business object operations also perform database management actions, retrieving and

	Component Fabrication	**Application Assembly**
Deliverable	Business Object Servers and Business Object Storage.	Application Modules. A working application on the user's desk top.
Rationale	Business objects are stable, recognisable software units that correspond to real-world entities. They are re-usable components, which can be built centrally or locally, and shared by all. Business objects offer services based on the data which they maintain about themselves.	Applications must be quick to build and change, but need to operate on shared, reliable data and rules. Applications can be built locally by 'assembling' business objects and GUI designs using front-end CASE tools. Application developers concentrate on supporting business processes & user tasks.
Development Tasks:	Project Definition, Domain Analysis, Business Object Storage Design, Build and Test, Installation and Data Conversion.	Project Definition, User Task Analysis, User Interface Design, Prototyping, Testing, Deployment.

Figure 3   The Two Streams of Component Based Development

storing the state (attribute-values and relationship pairings) of business objects. As explained earlier, we assume all business objects to be persistent. Business object servers can be built using declarative 4GLs, procedural 4GLs or object-oriented 3GLs. Central IS staff and department experts can build business object servers. Department staff would need the assistance of *component co-ordinators* to ensure that what they build has the correct level of generality and integrity, while central IS staff would need the assistance of domain experts, to ensure their components capture the required range of data items, rules and business policies.

The application modules contain user interface objects and are responsible for data validation, data preparation and invoking the business object operations. The developer must supply the 'glue' which assembles the application together from the business object components. The glue may be in the form of procedural logic or non-procedural rules entered as text, menu choices or graphically. Ideally it is the latter, since we intend that the department's own specialists and even end-users should be empowered to assemble their own applications. Having done this, they can progressively enhance their applications as they discover weaknesses in their solution, or as a response to new business requirements.

Building software in this way provides flexibility when using client-server platforms. The remote presentation, distributed function and remote data management styles, as defined in (Malik, 1991) are all feasible. The remote presentation style (see Figure 4) allocates both application modules and business object servers to a server (or host) processor. The distributed function style places the application modules on a work station (client processor), and business object servers on a server processor. The remote data style allocates both application modules and business object servers to a workstation, and relies on DBMS services to access remote, and possibly distributed, data storage.

Although business objects seem particularly suited to client-server developments, they are equally usable within batch and host-terminal environments. In batch applications, the application logic is concerned with validating the new data, matching data from multiple sources, and preparing reports; in host-terminal applications, the application logic validates the user input, presents data to the user and controls the conversation. In both cases, the updating of the shared databases, and the execution of standard business rules, are performed by the operations of business objects.

Both development streams must be executed to deliver meaningful systems[3], but there is a choice on how the streams inter work, as

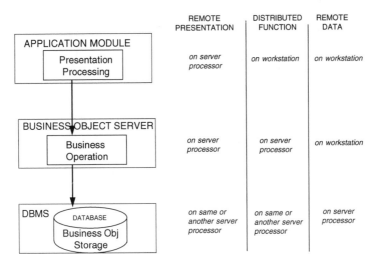

	REMOTE PRESENTATION	DISTRIBUTED FUNCTION	REMOTE DATA
APPLICATION MODULE — Presentation Processing	on server processor	on workstation	on workstation
BUSINESS OBJECT SERVER — Business Operation	on server processor	on server processor	on workstation
DBMS — DATABASE — Business Obj Storage	on same or another server processor	on same or another server processor	on server processor

Figure 4   Distribution Styles

illustrated in Figure 5. The rectangles represent development projects extending over time, which is represented by the horizontal axis.

The first strategy shown is termed *parallel development*. Two project teams work closely together—one producing the application, and the other the business objects needed by that application. The Component Fabrication team will aim to build business objects and operations that will be re-usable by other planned and unforeseen projects; but at the same time they cannot afford to seriously delay the application project they are paralleling. They may, then, need to postpone certain generalisations until after the application is implemented.

The second strategy has been termed *subsumed component fabrication*. In this arrangement, the Application Assembly team are expected to build

---

[3]Useful personal applications may, of course, be developed without the use of re-usable business objects. But sooner or later it will be seen that these applications embed useful business object types and rules which are likely to be beneficial to others. Sometimes the best and easiest solution is simply to pass a copy of that application to a colleague. But when shared data, rather than personal data is involved, it will be advantageous to separate out the business objects from such applications. Their state, rules and operations then become reusable in any number of applications. There can be a master copy of each business object accessible to all (who are authorised) and only 'one version of the truth' within a company.

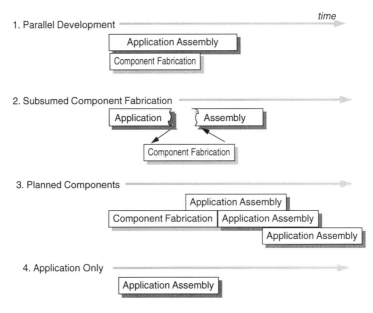

Figure 5   Progression Strategies

their own business objects or additional operations if they are not already available. A component co-ordination specialist would join the team to influence and advise on how the components are to be built. Many will consider this the most pragmatic approach, although the chances of application bias entering into business objects is higher. And this approach will be inappropriate within small application developments assembled by less technical departmental analysts.

The third strategy has been termed *planned components*. A 'library' of business object servers are designed, tested and generated prior to any application development. A database could be generated, ready to receive new objects, or this could wait until an appropriate application goes into production. This strategy requires the IS planning staff to determine which components are likely to be needed in the near-future—something which they can derive from their application development schedules. Component fabrication projects will typically componentise a business domain, such as accounting, ordering or personnel.

Domain models can be developed top-down, as advocated in traditional Information Engineering, or synthesised from current system descriptions. The server modules can be built from first principles, or opportunities for re-using legacy systems logic might be sought.

Depending upon the architecture of current systems, it may be possible to invoke operations embedded within existing modules directly. Another approach involves building object-based 'wrappers' (Graham, 1992) round entire existing systems, so the system itself acts as a super-component. While not conforming to the business object ideal, this does have the merit that existing (possibly hard to penetrate) code does not have to be interfered with. Re-engineering tools enable logic to be extracted from existing applications, and may prove useful when building components. In future, it should be possible to purchase business objects for specific industries, for inclusion in domain models or as executable modules or both.

The fourth strategy labelled application only should, in the fullness of time, be the *normal approach*. Once a critical mass of business object servers has been collected, application developments can go ahead without any corresponding Component Fabrication effort.

We envisage two broad classes of applications will be developed from components: pre-defined applications, and adaptable, *ad hoc* applications.

Pre-defined applications are appropriate when the business processes being automated are predictable and well-defined. Large-scale applications are put together in planned, formal Application Assembly projects, staffed by central IS developers assisted by end-users. But user departments can also take the initiative, and their own specialists can assemble local applications from the available components using non-technical CASE products, without reference to the central development function. Ideally, the end-users can subsequently customise the user interface— to suit their owns preferences and work situation.

We also propose a more *ad hoc* style of development needs to be available to computer literate end-users and department analysts. Development would proceed on an as-needed basis in response to local initiatives and day-to-day issues arising, so hardly warrants being termed a project. The resulting applications would be embedded within flexible desk-top tools like spreadsheets and word processors, and have the ability to link to, or contain replicas of, business objects. We envisage they can be built and readily changed in the run-time environment, in much the same way that a spreadsheet user can change the formulae in a spreadsheet at run-time. We use the term *adaptable application* to describe this end-user controlled combination of desk top tools and business objects.

The Development Context

The two streams of component-based development activity will be strongly influenced by other types of project.

A number of large corporations are now conducting *Business Process Re-engineering* projects which seek radical improvements in customer service, product quality and production costs. Besides demanding new applications, these projects typically delegate more decision-making to employees, who need access to corporate data and require flexible tools to fulfil their new responsibilities. The component-based approach should assist these employees to build their own decision support applications, and considerably shorten development lead times.

Central IS staff are sure to conduct some form of *Strategic Information Technology Planning*—to define a technical architecture, to define an enterprise systems development plan, to plan the provision of internal training and consultancy, and to generally co-ordinate systems development throughout the corporation. Strategic IT Planning is an ongoing task, although one-off studies will be carried out from time to time. This kind of planning work can help ensure that appropriate Component Fabrication projects are initiated in advance of critical application developments.

Figure 6 summarises these and other influences on the twin track approach. It shows that the corporate plans, objectives and strategies will influence the choice of BPR projects and the shape of the Strategic IT Plans. It shows that the main stimulus for Application Assembly is most likely to be new user requirements arising, and that the Strategic IT Plans

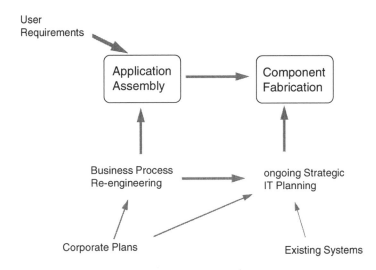

Figure 6   Principal Influences on the Component-Based Development Streams

are, to a fair extent, influenced by what applications and databases already exist.

Relationship to Information Engineering

The component-based development approach represents an evolution of Information Engineering towards a full-blown object oriented method for large-scale client-server information system development. It has been influenced by the work of the Object Interest Group, who recommend that "the OO approach involves two independent life cycles ... these are the component life-cycle and the application life-cycle" (Plant, 1991).

It has been shown that the Information Engineering methodology can be extended with object-oriented techniques: examples of such extensions can be found in Hutt (1994) and Short (1993). In this paper, component-based development, is primarily presented as a dual development life-cycle model, in which object-oriented, information engineering, and other structured development techniques could be all used. Component-based development's main focus is to build, buy or recover a collection of business object components, which can then be exploited within pre-defined or adaptable applications.

The components thus obtained could be standardised objects conforming to either the Object Management Group's Common Object Request Broker Architecture (CORBA) or Microsoft's Object Linking and Embedding (OLE), but could also be conventional modules which play the same role as objects. For a successful market in business objects to develop, international standards will needed. One body sharing this goal is the Business Object Management Special Interest Group (BOM SIG) of the Object Management Group.

THE ROLE OF CASE

CASE Requirements for Component-based Development

A combination of CASE products is required to support the component-based development approach. Ideally, a single product is able to support the Component Fabrication stream while a choice of products for Application Assembly seems appropriate. Figure 3 provides some indication on which development activities need supporting. A wide variety of diagramming techniques may be applied to these tasks, and we shall not attempt to enumerate them here. We would expect a CASE tool to support an integrated set of such techniques.

Component Fabrication demands a product that supports domain analysis and design through to business object module and database generation. It is also feasible for Component Fabrication to be supported by a combination of analysis and code generation tools, but these need to be well integrated. These tools will be used by system designers and business analysts, who do not necessarily work for the central IS function. Our view is that no programming should be involved; developers should be able to describe the domain and their design choices in diagrams, rules and option lists. Testing tools are essential: one approach would be to build a test application using Application Assembly products. Re-engineering tools, that enable objects or operations to be extracted from existing code, and wrapper building tools would also be beneficial within many organisations.

A variety of CASE solutions for Application Assembly is proposed. Pre-defined applications require tools to assist with User Task Analysis and Graphical User Interface Design. Many applications can then be assembled by simply selecting options from lists: event responses, input validation, output preparation and business object operation requests can be handled this way. More complex applications may require the assembly 'glue' to be built from procedural logic or non-procedural rules. Today, this may mean using tools like Visual Basic, but products which support non-procedural rules or icon-driven logic definition and diagrams of application behaviour would reduce the technical skills required and simplify maintenance. Assembly tools must allow the application to be developed iteratively: in particular, the potential end-users should be able try out the windows and dialogue paths before the business operation requirements and application logic have been defined.

The adaptable applications we referred to earlier require a different style of CASE support. The end-user would browse through the definitions of business objects in the repository, to define his or her own view of a group of business objects: the repository will explain the semantics of the objects' attributes, relationships and operations. This personal perspective of business data and processing can then be utilised from within a word processor, spreadsheet, presentation graphics or perhaps an icon-view of the world—such as that provided by NeWI from Integrated Objects (Ring, 1994). The CASE tools, then, provide the repository browsers and the interfaces that link the desk top tools up with the business object servers. The user could build, change and discard his personal perspectives, as required. The user works in the production environment: so no barrier exists between development and production environments. Equally, there is no barrier between developer and user. New applications and enhancements can be undertaken in hours rather than months. Once running successfully, they can be shared with colleagues. The use of business objects protects the integrity and security of the corporate data resource. The repository plays a key role: we suspect that a specialised run-time repository would be most efficient approach.

We maintain that application development without programming should be the norm: programming skills should only be needed for special situations. The application assemblers will, on the whole, be members of the department who require the application. Where end-users can build the application themselves, they should; else the department's own analysts should build the applications—they are already have the knowledge about their organisation unit's business processes, idiosyncrasies and priorities.

Repository Requirements

The essential foundation for all CASE support is, we suggest, an open *repository*. A repository is a database of system development information: domain models, business objects definitions, application designs, data storage designs and deployment details. Ideally, the repository will also store descriptions of legacy systems, business process re-engineering models and strategic IT models. Furthermore, development process models and project plans should also be included within the repository. The term repository does not have to mean a single physical database; the repository could be partitioned across a number of databases that play specialised roles; the repository could also be a distributed database. The essential thing is that the parts form a coherent whole which is accessible to all the tools.

The repository should be *open*—so that competing software suppliers can build a variety of tools that interwork via the repository, and it should be *extensible*—so the suppliers and users are not limited by pre-defined concepts.

The benefits of a repository-backed CASE approach are clear:

- it allows the sharing of information among users and developers
- it supports team-based, concurrent development activities
- it maintains accurate records of application configurations and where they are installed
- it maintains the catalogue of business objects
- it provides a mechanism for integrating a diversity of CASE tools

• it can enforce consistency—on an ongoing basis or on demand

• it provides secure storage for a vital resource.

We realise that the software industry's attempts to design such a repository have resulted in some miserable outcomes. But we contend that the arguments for an open, extensible repository is overwhelming. It is the repository that will maintain order in a fast changing world of innovative tools and rapidly built *ad hoc* applications.

Using Current CASE products

This section discusses the possibilities for using today's object-oriented CASE products for component-based application development.

A recent U.S. survey (Harmon, 1993) classified the object-oriented products into five categories, as shown in Figure 7[4]. The first two categories are sometimes termed 'top down' tools, while the lower three categories may be termed 'bottom-up'.

Many of the current crop of OO Analysis and Design Tools and I-CASE products can be used to build and document the object models— this being an essential stage within the Component Fabrication process. These models should define the attributes, relationships, integrity constraints and operations of the business objects of the domain. The I-CASE group of products can generate varying amounts of code for the business objects. They are typically able to generate business objects as C++ classes.

Application design and implementation are assisted in varying degrees by all categories of tool except the Analysis and Design Tools— these products do not usually support GUI design, even though they are classified as A&D tools. The Interface Development Tools assist the difficult task of GUI design and construction, but cannot really be considered as Application Assembly tools. The 4GL/Application Development Tools are usually able to build user interfaces and access relational databases. While this is a powerful combination, it hardly supports the vision of building applications from shareable business objects. We suspect that the widespread use of these tools will eventually result in a maintenance headaches for their owners. However, the use of an

---

[4]The report omits domain-specific OO tools and miscellaneous object-based tools. It excludes those European OO tools which were not available in the United States.

Category of Object Oriented Tool	Characterisation	Number in Category	Example
1. Analysis and Design Tools	- top-down in nature - allied to one or more OO methodologies or graphic notations of methodologies	13	Rational ROSE
2. I-CASE Products	- as (1) and.. - generates code, although this may be quite limited	16	Ptech
3. Interface Development Tools	- incremental, bottom-up tools; typically start by designing a UI; suits departmental developers - overlaps with UI class library and language environments - typically includes visual programming & UI painter to avoid direct working in language - many are specific to an OS—typically Windows 3.1	21	Open Interface 2.0
4. 4GL/Application Development Tools	- as (3), except ... - includes UI, DB manipulation and limited application development - usually generates SQL - sometimes supports client/server - application logic not usually OO	16	Power Builder
5. Advanced 4GL's	- for IS developers - for more complex applications than (4) - include graphical OO models - some originally positioned as expert systems, so include inferencing and pattern matching	6	ART Enterprise

Figure 7   Categories of Object-oriented CASE tool (based on Harmon, 1993)

I-CASE product for Component Fabrication, plus one of the bottom-up products that can build user interfaces and that can invoke the components looks to be a feasible option, although it does warrant further research.

Non object-oriented CASE tools could also be employed for component-based development. Although they will not generate business objects in object-oriented programming languages, it is quite possible to generate modules that offer business object operations. Here we can refer to a specific example—Texas Instruments' Information Engineering Facility (IEF) product. IEF provides tools suited to domain analysis; business object servers can be designed and generated by the IEF, based on the domain model operations. IEF also supports top-down Application Assembly. The application 'glue' is defined in action diagrams; the IEF generated application modules contain the IEF designed GUIs and send messages to the IEF fabricated business objects. The business objects' states are remembered in a relational database. Although different IEF toolsets are used within Component Fabrication and Application Assembly, its common repository is able to keep track of the business objects and how they are used in application designs. A common repository seems essential to ensure a measure of consistency and data integrity between the business objects and the application front-ends.

We suggest, however, that separate CASE products for Component Fabrication and Application Assembly would be advantageous. Different personnel, with varying individual levels of expertise and objectives will work on the two development streams, so products with different styles of interface, terminology and technical exposure would seem appropriate. Several products that all utilise a common repository appears to be the ideal arrangement. It would widen choice and not lock the buyer into one supplier. On the other hand bundling all capabilities up within a single complex I-CASE product would, one hopes, guarantee tool compatibility. Oberon's SynchroWorks is an example of a CASE product that conforms to the component-based philosophy; separate object fabrication and application assembly tools are included. Oberon's declared vision is one of computer-literate end-users being able to assemble their own personal productivity applications using visual editors.

CONCLUSION

Business object centred development is advocated for more than the usual 're-use reasons':

- it empowers department specialists and expert-users to develop their own applications that enjoy access to enterprise data and processing; at the same time the departments can be encouraged to make their data and processes available to others in the form of business objects

- it is business objects and their operations which differentiate companies, not their user interfaces and other technical objects

- it is particularly suited to client–server environments

- it supports adaptable, ad hoc applications: desk-top products become enterprise-data-enabled; applications can be changed by their user at run-time.

Companies should actively consider the twin-track approach to information systems development. A switch to this style of development is cultural as well as technical. It may be necessary to reward both the production and usage of business object components. Specialist component co-ordination staff are needed to promote and monitor component re-use.

The paper argues that a common repository is the essential enabling technology for component-based applications. This should be open and extensible. This will allow competitive CASE vendors to supply innovative solutions to application assembly and componentisation, and prevent corporations from being locked into one supplier. The repository would not just be used by central IS developers; it would be utilised by department application builders, and end-users building *ad hoc*, adaptable applications.

In the meantime, it should be possible to use the currently available object oriented and even non-OO CASE tools to begin this style of development.

In summary, the paper perceives that the dominant development pattern is changing to 'build, assemble, customise', and recommends that a CASE-assisted, component-based approach will play a key role in this transition. The goal is to reduce application development cycle times and enable employees to be more effective, by allowing them to 'grow their own' data processing services.

ACKNOWLEDGEMENTS

I am indebted to my colleague Bill Gibson for his assistance in preparing this paper.

REFERENCES

Booch G. 1994. *Object-Oriented Analysis and Design with Applications— Second Edition*. Benjamin Cummings.
Cox BJ. 1990. There is a Silver Bullet. *Byte Magazine*, October 1990.
Graham IM. 1992. Interoperation: Combining object-oriented applications

with conventional IT. *Object Magazine* **2**(4) SIGS Publications.

Harmon, P (ed.) 1993. Object-Oriented Development Tools. *Object Oriented Strategies*. **3**(6) Cutter Information Corp.

Hutt A. 1994. *Object Analysis and Design: Description of Methods*. QED/ Wiley.

Malik W, Percy A and Schulte R. 1991. *Client/Server and Co-operative Processing: A guide for the Perplexed*. Software Management Strategies, Gartner Group.

Plant N (ed.) 1991. *Object Orientation. An Assessment by Large Scale Users of Information Technology*. Object Interest Group, Kinver House, GU16 6PA.

Ring K. 1994. The Application is Dead: Long Live the Application. *Software Futures* **3**(4) APT Data Services.

Shelton RE. 1993. Object-Oriented Enterprise Modelling. *First Class* **2**(6); Object-Oriented Business Engineering. *First Class* **3**(3) Object Management Group.

Short K and Dodd J. 1993. Information Engineering with Objects. *Object Magazine* **3**(4) SIGS Publications.

Wilkie G. 1993. *Object-Oriented Software Engineering*. Addison-Wesley.

2

Developing Client-Server Systems Using OO Technology

Stuart Frost

ABSTRACT

CASE and methodology vendors have generally failed to help developers of information systems to meet rapidly changing business requirements. Given the current acceleration in the rate of change of those requirements (due to such trends as down-sizing and business process re-engineering), there is a clear need for a new approach to software development which can serve as the foundation for a new generation of CASE tools

This paper focuses on three key issues—the life-cycle, software architecture and development techniques—and brings them together to form a coherent approach to software development.

The approach, which mainly addresses the development of client server systems, has the following characteristics:

• Business processes are used to drive the analysis and design process.

Business Objects: Software Solutions. Edited by Kathy Spurr, Paul Layzell, Leslie Jennison and Neil Richards
© 1994 John Wiley & Sons Ltd

- A four schema architecture enables re-use of corporate objects and supports distributed systems.
- Object oriented techniques (drawn from Rumbaugh's Object Modelling Technique) are used to smooth and shorten the life-cycle.
- Incremental delivery is a key element of the life-cycle, as is iterative prototyping. Estimating is built into the life-cycle.

WHY DO WE NEED YET ANOTHER APPROACH TO SOFTWARE DEVELOPMENT?

In some parts of the IT industry—especially the trade press—CASE has been undervalued and misrepresented. This situation has arisen because businesses have been unable to justify in clear financial terms their investment in expensive tools and methodologies.

Several commentators have seen this as a vindication for approaches to software development which do not involve analysis and design phases —such as Rapid Application Development (RAD) using 4GLs and other GUI based development tools. Others have suggested that the methodologies are not comprehensive enough and have sought to make them ever more complex. Neither of these arguments is convincing.

Hacking away in a GUI builder can produce fast results, but unfortunately those results tend to be unpredictable (both in terms of meeting customer requirements and of meeting estimated delivery dates) and difficult to maintain. The scalability of such an approach is also questionable.

Complex methodologies such as SSADM, Booch and HP's Fusion, which rely on a large number of diagram types and a heavy textual context, are also unacceptable to the mainstream market which is, in general terms, demanding a more pragmatic, simplified approach to the problem.

What is needed is an approach which can be seen to help deliver results quickly in a controlled fashion. The key issues are as follows:

- *Business Processes*. Many businesses throughout the world are going through Business Process Re-engineering (BPR) at the moment and IT is seen as a key enabler. This is adding to the pressure to make IT development more responsive. It therefore makes sense to make support for business processes a central part of our approach to software development.
- *Architecture*. A rapid convergence on object technology is occurring in the software field. We will not be able to take advantage of the latest

computing technology (GUI builders[1], multi-media, OLE[2], CORBA[3], etc.) unless our software uses an object oriented architecture. This is discussed in more detail in a later section.

- *Code Re-use.* Most of the discussion concerning re-use has centred around class libraries. Although this is of course a very useful approach, it is not considered in detail in this paper. Rather, we will concentrate on the re-use of corporate objects in order to make a given project smaller and more predictable. However, this is not to say that the re-use of class libraries is excluded.

- *Iterative Life-cycle.* The traditional 'waterfall' model of software development requires 'completion' of each stage of software development before moving on to the next stage. This assumes that completion is an achievable target and potentially prolongs the life-cycle unnecessarily, in aiming for this target. An iterative life-cycle promotes faster delivery whilst providing a mechanism for incorporating changes. If we are to achieve our aim of developing IT systems which meet the needs of our business, we must use an iterative life-cycle.

  However, for an iterative life-cycle to work in practice, the stages of the life-cycle must be as few as possible and the differences between each of the stages must be small. In other words, we need a short, smooth life-cycle. Otherwise, the benefits of the approach are lost in the later stages of the project as we get bogged down with traceability problems.

  The incorporation of changes must also be easily achievable. Automation between the 'design and build' and the 'delivery' stages of the software life-cycle is therefore a major factor.

- *Prototyping and code generation.* If used sensibly, a good prototype can be of major benefit in discovering the users' requirements. By using a similar 'paradigm' in our analysis models and prototyping tools, we can achieve a high level of automatic code generation and thereby enhance and speed-up the (iterative) prototyping process.

- *Incremental Deliveries.* Many benefits accrue if we can deliver software in an incremental fashion:
  — Users of the system gain support for key aspects of their requirements much sooner than would otherwise be the case with

---

[1]GUI builders are software development tools such as Visual Basic or PowerBuilder which allow a developer to create a graphical user interface for (typically) a data base application.
[2]Object Linking and Embedding (OLE) is Microsoft's technology for allowing communication between different applications.
[3]Common Object Request Broker Architecture (CORBA) is a standard created by the Object Management Group to enable communication between objects across heterogeneous networks.

traditional waterfall developments.

— Management can see at a much earlier stage whether the IT department is able to deliver. This is often a significant factor in continued sponsorship.

— By breaking a system down into smaller increments, the development should be easier to manage.

However, attempts at adding incremental development to traditional structured methods have generally proved unsuccessful, due to the difficulty of choosing increments and subsequently integrating them.
Therefore, we need a well defined and controllable approach to incremental development.

- *Estimating.* Previous attempts at estimating software development projects in a repeatable fashion with acceptable accuracy have failed due to a dearth of good quality metrics which are applicable to most projects. This lack of metrics has occurred because of the wide variety of life-cycles and techniques in general use and because of the tendency to budget project by project, which causes project managers to take a very short term view ('Why should my project pay to produce metrics which benefit future projects?').

Summary

From the above, we can see that we need:

- An approach to software development which is centred on the support of business processes.
- A sound architecture which enables us to make use of and support the latest technology.
- A smooth life-cycle.
- A short life-cycle.
- The same paradigm in our analysis models as in our prototyping tools.
- The same paradigm in our design models as in our coding tools.
- A technique for estimating which benefits both current and future projects.

You may notice that object orientation is not listed. That's because we feel that it is an essential enabling technology which can act as a foundation for the achievement of the above aims. However, it is not an end in itself.

OVERVIEW OF A NEW APPROACH

There are three fundamental strands to the software development approach described in this paper—a software architecture which supports distributed client server systems, a life-cycle for software development which enables us to work in an iterative, incremental manner, and a set of graphical modelling techniques.

Architecture

Why do we need a better software architecture?

OK, it's bold assertion time—*Over the next two years, most software development projects will have to start using OO techniques.*

To understand why, we need to look beyond the usual arguments about re-use and inheritance and consider the future of computing architectures, especially those relating to client–server systems, i.e. distributed environments with a GUI front end.

It is generally true to say that most future systems will be distributed to some extent. This is not a new trend; there are various ways in which we can split the functionality of a system given current implementation technologies, for example dumb terminal linked to mainframe, PC linked to a file server, desktop client linked to a relational database server via SQL.

Ideally, we want the flexibility to distribute system functionality according to the actual requirements of our system and the business we are supporting, rather than at some arbitrary level set by software and hardware suppliers.

Such flexibility requires new technology, which is now starting to become available. Distributed object technology (e.g. CORBA and future versions of OLE) will allow us to distribute our applications across heterogeneous networks—providing that they are based upon an architecture which allows us to exploit such technology. The identification of objects is essential for this exploitation, but it will not be easy to choose the appropriate point to split an application. The benefits of distributed object technology in terms of performance and re-use of high level objects across a company will be very considerable.

This trend towards object technology will be accelerated by the widespread availability of Microsoft applications which are based on object linking and embedding (OLE), i.e. the latest versions of Word, Excel, etc. As users begin to appreciate the power and flexibility offered by this approach, they will start to demand the same level of functionality from packages developed in-house. They will also expect in-house systems to fully integrate with off-the shelf packages. This will only be possible if those in-house systems have an object-oriented architecture, because exploiting OLE technology without such an architecture is extremely difficult.

Other important factors in this convergence on object technology are: the trend towards multi-media applications, where the data complexity means that relational technology is not appropriate; and GUI builders which take an object-based approach, such as Visual Basic, PowerBuilder and SQLWindows.

Figure 1 shows an architecture which has been designed to exploit technologies such as OLE and CORBA. It also fits in well with the latest generation of GUI builders such as Visual Basic, whilst catering for relational storage technology where appropriate .

Let's take a look at each of the four layers (or 'schemata'):

- *User Interface (UI) Schema*
  This layer contains objects such as screens, menus and dialogs. It will therefore be highly dependent upon the implementation technology.
      Prototyping (using a tool such as Visual Basic) is the best way of designing the UI schema.
- *Local Schema*
  Local objects handle the *business requirements* of the project being

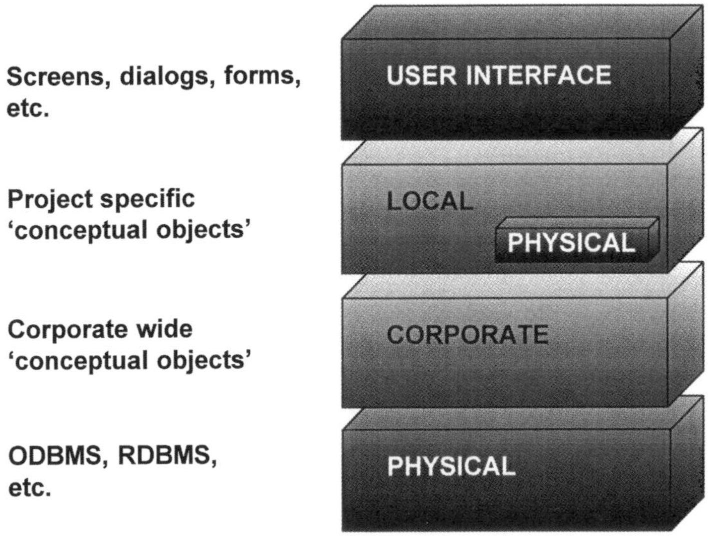

Screens, dialogs, forms, etc.	USER INTERFACE
Project specific 'conceptual objects'	LOCAL / PHYSICAL
Corporate wide 'conceptual objects'	CORPORATE
ODBMS, RDBMS, etc.	PHYSICAL

Figure 1   Four Schema Architecture for OO Systems

developed. It is important to maintain a clear distinction between the technology-dependent user interface layer and the needs of the business. Objects in this layer (and the corporate layer discussed below) are sometimes referred to as *conceptual* or *business entity objects*.

If local storage is needed, there should be further separation between the needs of the business and the technology dependent physical storage (see below).

- *Corporate Schema*

Corporate level objects contain functionality and data which is relevant to the whole organisation.

Firm 'contracts' should be made between the providers of corporate objects and the users of those objects on specific projects. It is also very useful if the teams responsible for the creation of corporate objects are required to provide off-line equivalents of those objects for prototyping and testing purposes.

The separation between local and corporate objects gives great potential for high levels of re-use across an organisation. In addition, if we base projects on a sound corporate schema, considerably less work is required for each project. This eases the application of such techniques as rapid application development and means that our project teams can be smaller. When we put these two factors together (i.e. re-use of corporate objects and smaller projects), very large gains in productivity are possible.

For very large systems, the Corporate Schema may be subdivided into further layers, but this is not relevant from the point of view of a given project, since only the top-most layer will be seen.

- *Physical Schema*

The Physical Schema encapsulates the storage of data, which may be in a relational or object database.

If, as is generally the case with current systems, relational technology is used, we will need to deal with the mapping between the objects in the local and corporate schema and the relational tables. As long as our objects are relatively simple, this does not create too many problems. However, applications which need to handle complex objects (e.g. multi-media) will be easier to implement in an object database such as Object Store. The mapping to the physical layer is then much more straightforward.

The above description illustrates the 'client-server' relationship between the various layers. The various schema boundaries therefore represent a good first choice when considering points at which to distribute systems.

However, we must also take into account the frequency of messages passing between the objects and the amount of data which is handled by each message.

An Iterative, Incremental Life-Cycle

Key elements of the life-cycle are:

- Business processes form a continuous thread through the life-cycle.

- It uses OO techniques to give a smooth, short life-cycle.

- It uses event driven techniques.

- It is iterative.

- Prototyping is integrated into the methodology from the beginning.

- It supports incremental delivery.

- Estimating is taken into account and can be carried out at several stages in the life-cycle.

As shown in Figure 2, the life-cycle starts with a feasibility study which allows us to assess the likely costs and complexity of the project. It then progresses to a business study stage which uses prototyping as an integral part of the analysis process. Once we have a good overall picture of the scope and complexity of the users' requirements, we can choose which part (or increment) of the system to deliver first and carry out detailed analysis and design of the relevant objects.

There are two iteration loops in the life-cycle—one at the business study phase, where we need close coupling between the analysis model and the prototype; and the second between the detailed design and the delivery of a given increment.

By keeping the life-cycle smooth and short, we can minimise the integration problems as each increment is delivered.

Later sections will discuss each stage of the life-cycle in greater detail.

Graphical Modelling Techniques

The techniques used within the life-cycle are mainly drawn from Rumbaugh's (1991) OMT, and consist of the following diagram types:

- *Object Diagrams*. These show the various classes (or object types) in

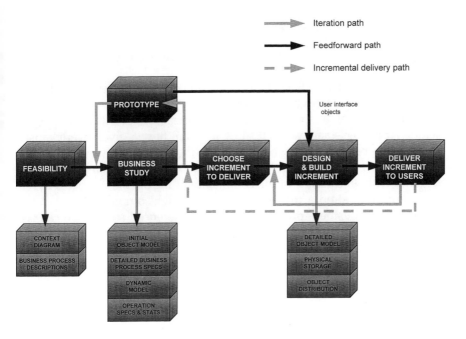

Figure 2 Life-Cycle Diagram

the system and the relationships between them. The syntax is identical to that used in OMT and is very expressive and powerful.

- *State Transition Diagrams.* These show how each object responds to events. The syntax is again the same as that used in OMT, although the inheritance of dynamic behaviour from a super class is handled in a more defined way.

- *Object Interaction Diagrams.* These show how a business process is supported by means of messages passing between objects.

FEASIBILITY STUDY

What Are We Trying To Achieve At This Stage?

- To scope the project
- To find out who/what the project will interact with

- To assess whether we can afford to go ahead

To achieve the above aims, we use catalogues of actors on the system and business processes.

The Actor catalogue lists all of the people or other systems which may interact with the system being analysed.

Business processes show how the system reacts to events generated by actors. At a later stage, we will show in detail how a given event causes messages to be passed between objects in the system. However, for now we will need to give a textual description of each business process, together with an estimate of the complexity of the business process in relative terms (e.g. simple, medium complexity, high complexity).

Actors and business processes are cross-referenced so that we can see who/what invokes a given business process.

BUSINESS STUDY

What Are We Trying To Achieve At This Stage?

The primary aim is to make sure we know what the users want. Secondary aims are:

- To provide a sound basis for later incremental development

- To gain an understanding of the business processes required from corporate level objects

- To refine our estimates

To achieve the above aims, we start by having a first-cut at creating an initial object model, then move on to specify the business processes in more detail. From this activity, we will be able to further identify and confirm objects and operations on those objects, thus adding to the initial object model.

Thus, the specification of business processes and the creation of an initial object model are very closely intertwined, and become an iterative process (see Figure 3).

The dynamics of each of the objects in the model are then specified, together with the inputs and outputs of each of the operations.

Prototyping is the best way of testing our analysis model with users. It should be an integral part of the analysis process, not an afterthought, feeding information into the various components of the analysis model.

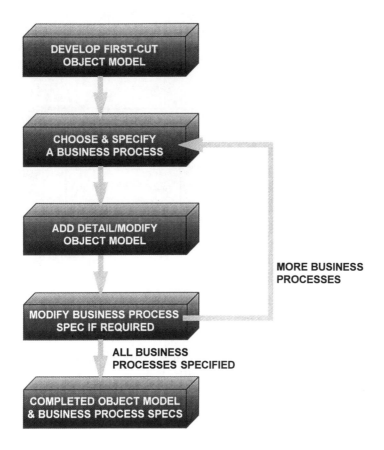

Figure 3   Iteration Between Business Process Specification and Object Modelling

The business study is intended to be a relatively short phase of the project. We should not expect to specify every part of the system to a minute level of detail. Rather, we are trying to take a step towards gaining a better understanding of the user requirements. More detail will be added at the later, incremental stage of the project.

Initial Object Model

The object model uses Rumbaugh's OMT notation, which has become

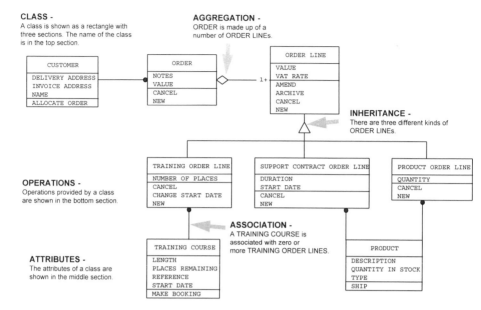

Figure 4   Object Model Example

established as the most popular way of showing classes and the relationships between those classes (see Figure 4).

Business Processes

To specify the business processes, we will create Object Interaction Diagrams (OID) which show how an event (i.e. the starting point of a business process) causes messages to pass between the objects in our system.

An OID explicitly shows the operation which is called on each object. It also highlights aggregations (via the * symbol) and inheritance structures (via the **o** symbol)[4].

---

[4]This symbology is drawn from that used in Jackson structure charts and should therefore be well known by most analysts and programmers. The asterisk implies repetition and is used where an object is made up of one or more parts (i.e. an aggregation). This means that the message must be sent to each of the parts. The circle implies selection and is used where a given message must be directed to the appropriate sub-type. Note that in some implementations, this could be handled by polymorphism.

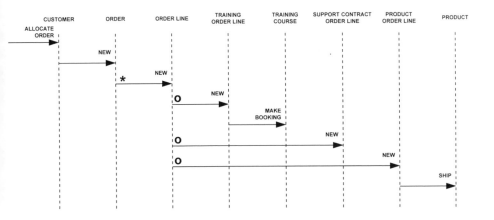

Figure 5   OID for ORDER PROCESSING

When specifying a business process using an OID, the analyst has to decide how much detail is required concerning exceptions. If every exception is shown in great detail, the user may be overwhelmed— and the business study may never be finished! There is a clear trade-off between confusing the user at the business study phase and running the risk of finding misunderstandings at the incremental delivery phase. OID drawing tools can help by providing facilities to support folding and hierarchical breakdown.

Sequencing may also be detailed on the OIDs, using Dewey Decimal numbers (1, 1.1, 1.2, 1.2.1, 2, 2.1, etc.). The frequency of each message should also be recorded to assist later decisions regarding potential distribution of the system across a network.

Prototyping should form an integral part of the specification process for business processes, with iteration between the prototype and the analysis models. The prototyping tool should also be used to specify the user interface objects such as screens, forms and dialogs. Close integration is therefore required between the tools used for creating the analysis models (i.e. SELECT) and those used for prototyping (e.g. Visual Basic).

Dynamic Model

Dynamic modelling illustrates the behaviour of a given object when it receives messages (via calls to operations).

The dynamic modelling notation is drawn from Rumbaugh's OMT and uses state transition diagrams (see Figure 6).

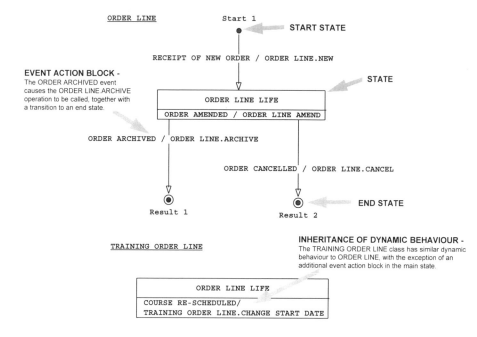

Figure 6   STDs for the Order Line Inheritance Structure

The State Transition Diagram (STD) for TRAINING ORDER LINE shows how the single state in the parent class' STD is modified. All other transitions and actions are the same, so they are not shown. STDs for the remaining classes in the structure are identical to that for ORDER LINE and are therefore not drawn.

Operation Specifications & Statistics

For each of the operations identified in the object model, we need to specify the volume of data which will be input and output on each invocation. Together with the frequency information detailed on the Object Interaction Diagrams, this will assist in decisions concerning the distribution of objects.

We will also need to provide a textual description of each operation. Pseudo code can be used for this purpose if preferred.

CHOOSE, DESIGN & BUILD AN INCREMENT

What Are We Trying To Achieve At This Stage?

Primary Aims
- To deliver usable functionality to users as quickly as possible
- To satisfy management that we can meet the requirements of the business

Secondary Aim
- To refine our estimates for the remaining increments

Choosing Increments

In the past, some methods developers have suggested splitting the data (or object) model up to form a basis for incremental development. This is usually carried out by minimising the number of relationships which cross increment boundaries. Unfortunately, because such an approach does not take direct account of the functionality required by users, it can lead to arbitrary divisions of user requirements across incremental deliveries.

As they are directly representative of the user requirements, business processes form a much better basis for choosing increments.

It is obviously very important to keep users and management 'on our side' throughout the development process. The easiest way of doing this is to deliver the juiciest increments first. To put this another way, look for the best ratio of high value to low cost, so that we can deliver a good level of functionality as quickly as possible.

A key question to ask is—how *little* can we spend in return for delivering the maximum value to users? Traditional development methods turn this round and ask—how *much* can we achieve given some critical constraint (e.g. time, cost, etc.)? (Gilb, 1988).

It is probable that some business processes are more critical to the operation of the business than others. The business process approach also enables the incremental delivery to be prioritised on the basis of need.

Designing Increments

When designing an increment (i.e. software to support a given business process), we need to provide appropriate functionality on each of the objects which are utilised as the business process is supported by the system.

We also need to add more detail concerning exceptions to the Object Interaction Diagrams.

In addition, we will need to look at how the provision of the business process is to be controlled. In general terms, we want to separate the functionality provided by a given object from the control of the object. This enhances the re-usability of objects, since the same functionality may be required in a later project, but in a different order, or at different times.

We also need to consider how the data held by each object is going to be stored. If we use an object database (ODBMS), the mapping between the object model and the database is likely to be straightforward, since an ODBMS is designed to directly handle the complex data structures and relationships which are present in an object model—although we may have to consider some performance optimisation.

However, a relational database (RDBMS) is not so easy to handle. We may need to use an RDBMS in an OO system for a variety of reasons:

- Large amounts of corporate data may be stored in an RDBMS such as Oracle.

- The company standard database may be relational.

- We may feel that ODBMS technology is not yet mature enough— especially in the area of end-user query tools.

When considering the problem of mapping between an object model and an RDBMS, we therefore need to look at the issue from two angles:

1. *Mapping a new design onto a fresh set of tables*
    The main problem areas in this case are keys, object complexity and inheritance structures.

    Keys are not relevant in an object model, since the objects in a given class automatically have unique identity—even though they may contain the same data. In an OO environment, this is implemented via pointers or some other system generated addressing mechanism. However, relational technology requires the specification of a key. Therefore, we must either identify a key from one or more of the attributes of an object, or we must introduce a unique reference attribute for use as a key.

    A given object may be too complex to store in a single table. Hence, we must be able to map a single object onto multiple tables.

    Because inheritance is not supported by relational databases, we will need to decide whether the sub-classes are to be 'rolled-up' into

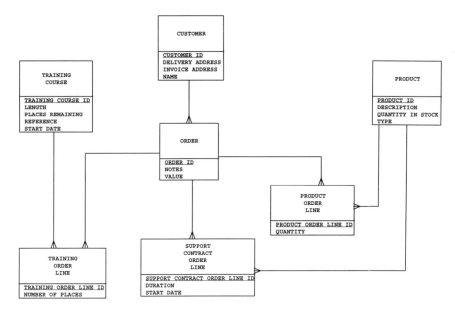

Figure 7   Physical Data Structure for Order, etc.

a single table representing the superclass, or the superclass is to be 'rolled-down' into each of the sub-classes.

The object model is first converted to a set of 'ideal' tables (Rumbaugh, 1991). These tables represent common characteristics of RDBMS. This 'first-cut' physical design can then be refined according to more specific design and optimisation requirements, and to take account of any special features of the target RDBMS.

There are a number of mapping alternatives. Any class may map to one or more relational tables. Rumbaugh describes two ways in which to map an association to tables, and four ways to map an inheritance structure or generalisation. The following rules provide conversion mapping at its simplest level:

(i)   an object class maps to a table

(ii)   an association maps to a table

(iii) a generalisation maps to a superclass table plus a series of sub-class tables.

The alternative mappings presented in Rumbaugh (1991) trade off performance, integrity and extensibility.

2. *Mapping a set of existing tables to an object model so that we can access the data from our new system*
    In this case, we will need to encapsulate each of the tables within one or more classes and then provide access routines on each class so that the data is made available to the rest of our application.

In both cases, we can represent the relational tables and the relationships between them by using an entity relationship diagram, as used in most structured methods.

Building Increments

Due to the nature of the models built during previous stages, CASE vendors such as ourselves will be able to provide a very high level of code generation. This will typically include automatic generation of the class structures and state machine management routines, hooks into relational databases (via, for example, ODBC—Open Database Connectivity—and generation of SQL schema), and interfaces to pre-defined CORBA and OLE objects.

The code generation facilities should go further than the current one-pass tools, and include support for re-generation of code, so as to enable iteration between the design and the final application.

In addition, the user interface objects which were developed during the prototyping stage can be passed over to the final application, either directly if the same GUI builder is to be used, or via a translator where possible and appropriate.

The main manual task at this stage will be to transform the textual descriptions of operations into the target code.

Integration problems as each increment is delivered should be minimised because we already have a sound overall view of the whole system from the business study stage.

ESTIMATING

At the feasibility stage, it is possible to base an estimate on the complexity of the business processes, using a modified form of Function Point Analysis (FPA). It is important to note that we cannot expect a high level of accuracy! However, over time, our analysts will build up sufficient experience in the techniques to at least give us something better than the usual 'finger in the air' approach. As we will see later, the estimates can also be refined as we work through the development of the project.

Once the Business Study is complete, we will have a much greater understanding of the complexity of the Business Process specification, together with knowledge of the object model. We can therefore revise our estimates using a similar, modified form of FPA to that discussed in the feasibility section.

As each increment is completed, we have an opportunity to revise the estimates for the remaining increments based on actual results. The data can also be used for other projects, so that future estimates should be more reliable.

There is a clear opportunity here for CASE vendors such as ourselves to 'close the loop' by integrating with estimating and project management packages, so that actual results can be automatically fed-back so as to improve the estimates.

CASE SUPPORT FOR THE METHOD

Select Software Tools Ltd have developed a comprehensive workbench to support the approach described in this paper.

The graphical techniques (object diagrams, state transition diagrams and object interaction diagrams) together with the various catalogues (e.g. of actors and business processes) are supported by an enhanced version of our SELECT/OMT toolkit, which is itself a member of our well established range of Windows-based CASE tools.

Comprehensive support for the life-cycle has been provided by integrating the SELECT toolkit with Microsoft Word (for document generation), Excel (for estimating) and Project (for project management). This integration is carried out via an open OLE interface to SELECT.

In addition, iterative prototyping facilities are provided in Visual Basic, and comprehensive code generation is being developed for Visual C++, using Visual Basic for the GUI portion of a client-server application.

CONCLUSIONS

Although most of the issues discussed in this paper (RAD, prototyping, iterative life-cycles, incremental delivery, multi-layer architecture, estimating, OO techniques, etc.) have been used individually in previous development methodologies, we believe that this is the first time they have been brought together in a coherent approach which can be used by the majority of IT developers.

The methodology also lends itself to CASE support, because the diagrams are already supported by several vendors, and additional aspects such as estimating and project management can be added via integration with third-party programs (this is much easier to achieve than in the past now that interfaces such as OLE are widely supported).

It certainly seems that OMT as described by Rumbaugh is now the most popular set of OO techniques. By extending the techniques slightly and placing them within a comprehensive methodology, we believe that a significant step forward has been achieved in terms of bringing OO technology into the mainstream of software development.

REFERENCES

Coleman D et al. 1994. *Object-Oriented Development: The Fusion Method*. Prentice Hall.

Gilb T and Finzi S. 1988. *Principles of Software Engineering Management*. Addison-Wesley.

Jacobson I. 1992. *Object-Oriented Software Engineering: A User Case Driven Approach*. ACM Press.

Rumbaugh J et al. 1991. *Object-Oriented Modelling and Design*. Prentice Hall.

3

Progress in CASE Support for Software Development Methods

Allan S. Kennedy, Adrian F. King and Ian T. Wilkie

ABSTRACT

In the process of providing consultancy support to a large number of projects during the 1980s and early 1990s we observed an increasing user dissatisfaction with the then existing CASE products. As a result, we performed a fundamental review of the aims and implementation of system development methods and the CASE tool support for them. This re-evaluation enabled us to detail the ways in which the existing products failed, and therefore outlines the way forward for achieving a higher level of support in the future.

To meet the demands of major system development projects, tool developers must understand and support development methods that are rigorous and have complete life-cycle coverage. To provide useful support, the way in which analysts and designers work together within an organisation must be understood. Together with the correct choice of

Business Objects: Software Solutions. Edited by Kathy Spurr, Paul Layzell, Leslie Jennison and Neil Richards implementation strategy the resulting products can offer a level of support unheard of with the existing products.

The outcome of this work has been the development of *Intelligent OOA*, a new CASE product that offers rigorous method support and seamless life-cycle transitions. The product has already been used with success on a number of recent large system development projects.

INTRODUCTION

During the 1980s, CASE products were being adopted in all areas of system development, and considerable investment in the technology was made by organisations, with variable returns.

For most of this time, members of Kennedy Carter consulted to, and worked on, many projects that used structured and object oriented software development techniques. These projects were concerned with a variety of application domains such as Telecommunications, Air Traffic Control, Naval Command and Control, Avionics, Flight Simulation, Industrial Process Control, Travel Reservation and Accounting, Optical Scanning and High Energy Particle Accelerators. In these projects, the use of CASE products was a significant factor.

In seeing CASE applied to these projects, we observed that the products had short-comings, and that users were becoming increasingly demanding. These observations were echoed in published articles (Jones, 1992; Davenport, 1992).

As a result, we undertook a fundamental review of the aims and implementation of system development methods and the CASE tool support for them. This work enabled us to understand the reasons for the problems being experienced, and put us in an ideal position to specify and develop a new product for the 1990s.

The Requirements for a CASE Tool

The aim of a CASE tool, should be to aid the analyst/designer in the activity of creating or maintaining an automated system. To assess the effectiveness of CASE tools in meeting this aim, it is relevant to examine the nature of the system development process itself.

The process of system development is one that starts with an initial idea for a product and proceeds through a number of stages until the product is delivered. The process continues with the maintenance of the product in service. A typical paradigm of the 1970s and 1980s is shown in Figure 1.

These activities could be characterised as follows:

- *Analysis*: the process of understanding the nature of a problem without regard to how it may be solved.

- *Design*: the process of evolving a cost effective solution to the problem, that delivers adequate performance and reliability.

- *Implementation*: the process of constructing the solution by following the design evolved in the previous step.

- *Maintenance*: the process of fixing defects in the delivered products, adjusting the product to respond to changes in the environment and of responding to new or changed requirements.

The descriptions of each phase are necessarily vague for two reasons:

1. They relate to the general outline of many development processes, without addressing any one in particular.

2. In practice, there is often only a vague idea about the precise nature and aim of each phase, even when applied to a specific project.

In fact, there are almost as many opinions as to what the various stages of system development are and should be as there are systems engineers. To satisfy such a variety of opinion it is almost impossible for any CASE tool to provide more than the most rudimentary sort of support, such as document production facilities.

Clearly, it is necessary to impose some order on this situation. One solution is to adopt a 'standard' system development method such as

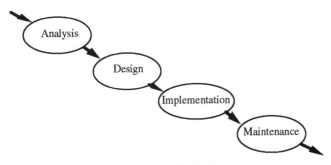

Figure 1 Typical System Development Life-Cycle

SSADM or Real Time Structured Analysis and Structured Design (RTSASD) (DeMarco, 1978; Ward & Mellor 1985-86; Page-Jones, 1980). Methods such as these define a particular development life-cycle, specifying the nature of each phase, the deliverables of each phase and techniques for executing each phase. This involves specification of notations for presenting information about the system and rules for the use of the notation that aid legibility and help to ensure the internal consistency of the information.

For example, Ward-Mellor RTSASD specifies the following series of deliverables:

1.   The 'Essential Model', consisting of:
     • Context Diagram
     • Information Model
     • Event List
     • Behavioural Model (Data Flow Diagrams and State Transition Diagrams)

2.   The 'Implementation Model', consisting of:
     • Processor Environment Model
     • Software Environment Model
     • Code Organisation Model

where each element of the various models has a defined structure, and should conform to a defined set of rules.

We are now in a position to define a minimal set of requirements for a CASE tool supporting a system development method:

1.   Support for the notations of a specific development method.

2.   Support for enforcing the rules of the method.

3.   Support for teams of analysts and designers working together on a project.

4.   Hypertext navigation facilities through the database.

However, system development is not just a series of isolated steps. Each step depends upon, and utilises the understanding provided by, the previous step. For example, we perform analysis to understand the problem, so that the design stage can evolve a system that solves the *same* problem. In other words, system development can be viewed as a series of transformations from initial requirements or problem statements, through analysis and design into code and the delivered system. Some methods even go so far as to propose specific transformation strategies from one stage to the next. For example, since its earliest days, Structured Design has promoted a series of strategies for transforming data transformation networks (Data Flow Diagrams) into code module calling hierarchies (Structure Charts). This would be applied in order to evolve the 'Code Organisation Model' in RTSASD.

It is reasonable to expect that a CASE tool will aid the system developer in these activities. Further, since these transformations apply from the earliest textual documents right through to the delivered system, the development environment should cover the entire life-cycle, and help us keep track of what transformations have been applied (whether automatic or analyst produced), and what the results of the transformation were. Our requirements list should thus be augmented to include support for transitions between development life-cycle phases:

5.   Automatic transformations between one stage and the next where possible.

6.   Support for all life-cycle stages from Requirements to Code.

7.   Support for maintenance of traceability information.

Finally, although development methods assist the developer in producing internally consistent models of the system, they do not guarantee it. Neither do they guarantee that an internally consistent model agrees with the reality of the real world problem it is trying to represent. These issues must be addressed by testing.

This leads to the requirements:

8.   Support for checking and testing of the internal self consistency of models.

9.   Support for the testing of model statements against the real world problem.

The Capabilities Of Existing CASE Tools

How then do CASE tools match up to these expectations? The answer is, unfortunately, that many existing and even recent products do not meet these requirements well. In the following section we will detail some of they ways in which products fail. In doing so we do not claim that no product meets any of the goals—far from it. Many products excel in certain areas, and others achieve reasonable broad support.

We will now outline some of the problem areas.

Many existing products focus on the notations themselves, rather than the methods that the notations support.

These tools will allow the analyst virtually any freedom, since most details are supplied at the level of free text.

The tool may store knowledge of the same idea in several places. This in itself is not a problem except that it is usually the responsibility of the user to maintain the various copies of the information. At most, the tool will provide checking facilities to warn if the copies are out of step. This situation can develop into a configuration management nightmare.

For example consider two possible representations of a finite state machine: The State Transition Diagram and The State Transition Table. Each provides a different insight into the problem being described, and ideally a tool would allow the user to enter information in either representation and allow him to see the results in the other. However, in practice few tools exhibit this capability. Instead, the user must maintain two separate diagrams himself.

Multiuser support is often very limited and amounts to little more than a multiuser database. There is little support for the idea of analysts working in teams where changes to model elements must be controlled and coordinated. Where such control is supplied it usually focuses on the access to diagrams, rather than the under-lying information. Two analysts may thus change the same fact at the same time.

Another feature of the current generation of products is that each one will often attempt to deal only with a limited part of the development life-cycle. To cover the whole life-cycle, a user will typically have to purchase a number of different products from different vendors. The resulting lack of integration can have a significant impact on the usability of the development environment.

Many Analysis/Design tools have a very limited approach to configuration management and simply provide an interface to allow export of data to and import of data from an external configuration management product. Limited facilities are then provided to utilise configuration management within the scope of the analysis and design effort. Similarly, if we wish to tackle Requirements Traceability, Testing or Simulation, then we are likely to have to integrate several different products together.

Very few products achieve a useful level of support for transforming from one stage of the system development process to the next. Potentially, this is where we might expect CASE tools to provide the biggest productivity gains with the ultimate possibility of complete system generation from analyses or designs held in the database. Of course, there are products that do achieve significant worthwhile support, but these do so only for a limited set of system architectures. For example, in the information system sector, much success has been achieved. However, large scale code generation for real-time embedded systems where functionality must be distributed across multiple tasks in multiple processors while still achieving tight performance constraints has so far remained an unsatisfied goal. The reasons for this are twofold:

- When examined closely, many of the existing analysis methods have ambiguities in their operational semantics rendering the task of *systematic* transformation to a system design and to code very difficult, if not impossible to achieve.

- To support the generation of systems with complex and sophisticated real-time architectures, the nature of system architectures and transformations from analysis formalisms must be understood.

In summary, existing products while achieving much, fail in a number of respects:

- Typical single products address only part of the development lifecycle. Some products achieve a high degree of success in their own area, but for a comprehensive development environment, the user must integrate a number of offerings from different vendors. Individual products, however, lack the overview of the whole development process. This leads to the phenomenon of 'islands of automation'. Each island may function well on its own, but bridging the void from one to another is difficult.

- Even within a single 'island', many products do not live up to user expectations of them.

In short, the existing CASE offerings do not address the fundamental goal of aiding the whole process of system development. They fail to understand that there is 'a system for building systems' which must be supported.

As a result, organisations who have made significant investments in CASE technology find that the returns fall far short of their expectations.

RECURSIVE DEVELOPMENT

Since our requirements indicate that a CASE tool should provide support for a specifc method we must make sure that we choose a suitable one. There are two key issues in the choice:

- The method must address the whole development life-cycle and, in particular, must address the issues involved in building different system architectures.

- Analysis and design formalisms must be sufficiently rigorous and precise so as too allow the possibility of systematic transformation from one development stage to the next.

One method that meets these criteria is Recursive Development (RD) (Shlaer and Mellor, 1988, 1990,1992; Carter and Raistrick, 1992). RD is a system development process which can be summarised as shown in Figure 2.

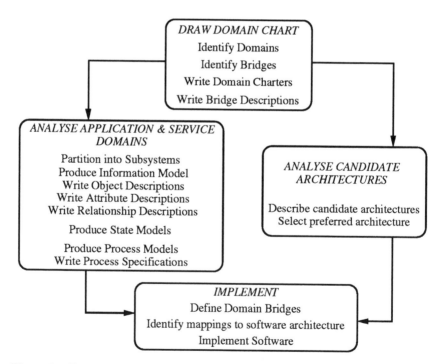

Figure 2   Recursive Development Life-Cycle

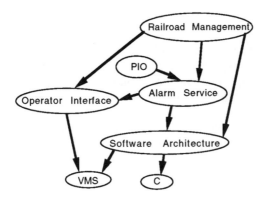

Figure 3 Domain Chart

Domain Partitioning

Domains are distinct subject matter areas which can and should be analysed separately. The Domain Chart (Figure 3) provides a graphical summary of the chosen domains and their dependencies.

The dependencies are represented here by broad arrows between domains. One domain depends on another when it requires the use of services provided by that domain. The direction of the arrow 'points to' the domain providing the service. The arrow thus represents a 'bridge' between two domains that must be specified so as to indicate exactly how the service required by the client domain is matched to one provided by the client domain.

By using this separation of concerns, analysts can concentrate on the subject matter of, for example, graphical user interfaces, without being concerned about the use to which the domain is being put. Of course, domains cannot be analysed in total isolation, since they must provide the services that are required of them by higher level domains. However, by careful use of generalisation, a specific requirement from a client domain ('display train status summary') can be transposed to a more re-usable service in the client domain ('display text line in window'). This can form the basis for reuse of software on a large scale. Rather than reusing individual components, entire domains consisting of interacting objects can be reused as a whole. The emphasis when searching for software to reuse is on 'what services do I require', rather than 'what objects are available that might do what I want?'

Domain Analysis

Although, in principle, we could choose any analysis formalism to describe a domain, there is a constraint. The formalism must be sufficiently precise that mappings can be defined from the components of the analysis notation onto components of the chosen software architecture. Object Oriented Analysis is such a formalism.

For the purposes of performing recursive development, domains are categorised into four groups:

1. *Application Domain*
    The analysis of the application domain is comparable to the ideas of logical or essential models from earlier analysis and design methods (DeMarco, 1978; Ward and Mellor, 1985/6). The purpose of the analysis of the application domain is to capture knowledge and understanding of the problem being considered. The subject matter is that of the end user and not the system developer.

2. *Service Domains*
    Service domains represent subject matters which are largely independent of the application but which are required to support it. Examples of common service domains include:

    *   *Operator Interface*: it is possible and desirable to formalise the characteristics and behaviour of screens, windows, icons, scroll bars and so on without alluding to the application to be supported.

    *   *Physical Input/Output*: at a low level this domain typically comprises input and output registers, analogue-to-digital and digital-to-analogue converters.

    *   *Alarms*: many systems have a requirement to inform operators of alarm conditions.

    *   *Recording & Playback*: this domain provides services to permit recording of transactions, events and user interactions for later playback and analysis.

    As we outlined before, and can be seen from this set of examples, service domains provide potential for reuse at a high level. This is because they are not polluted with knowledge of the application that will use their services. The purpose of analysis in the service domains is not always the same as in the application domain.

Analysis of the application domain develops an understanding of the real world, whereas analysis of a service domain may require the creation of an abstract world. The analysis in these circumstances states the policies of that abstract world for others to understand. The development of an innovative operator interface would fall into this category. Of course, the subject matters of some service domains, for example communications protocols, may be clearly defined in published standards and creativity on the part of the analyst is neither required nor permitted

3. *Software Architecture Domain*
   This domain is covered in more detail below.

4. *Implementation Domains*
   Implementation domains typically include programming languages, run-time systems and operating systems. These are rarely subjected to a formal analysis, as they are usually detailed in reference manuals and standards. It is important, however, to have a good understanding of the facilities provided by the implementation domains because elements of the other domains will utilise these domains.

Object-Oriented Analysis

OOA is a formalism for analysing the content of any domain. It is found-

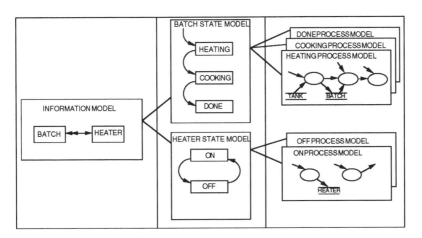

Figure 4   OOA Model Organisation

ed upon the well established notion of three viewpoints used, but these viewpoints are more convincingly integrated than has been the case in previous methods. While the three views (information, dynamics and process) are expressed with familiar RTSA notations, they are tightly integrated into a model structure which owes more to JSD (Sutcliffe, 1988). Figure 4 shows the OOA model structure.

Each object (analogous to an entity in other methods) which has dynamic behaviour will have a state model (or entity life history). The Moore finite state model is used which specifies processes to be executed on entry to each state. Therefore, a process model can be developed for each state showing the data dependencies between the processes in that state. In many cases, however, the actions specified in the state models require no further elaboration.

The relative importance of the three viewpoints is quite clear: the information model takes priority, the state model is second and the process model is relegated to third place. This simply reflects the capacity of the notations to describe large and complex subject matters clearly. Note that the analyst does not have the discretion to build or organise the models in any other way. This contributes significantly to the precision of analysis models built with OOA.

The Software Architecture

The software architecture domain proclaims and enforces system-wide rules defining the organisation and access of data and the overall control of the system as a whole. The software architecture can also be viewed as a virtual machine layer which isolates the application and service domains from the implementation domains. This can be seen on the domain chart (Figure 3).

The architecture domain is not real-world based. It is created by proficient designers and is potentially very reusable. By stating and enforcing system-wide policies it is possible to create uniform, coherent and consistent designs. Architectures can be compared, contrasted, measured and tuned to ensure compliance with performance and resource requirements. The system developer can have a set of architectures to choose from, each with particular characteristics: some highly fault tolerant, some optimised for high speed responses to stimuli.

Object oriented architectures are one class of architecture that can be produced from OOA. In these architectures we can exploit such features as inheritance and polymorphism to implement the system. For example, inheritance can be use to implement single run time classes that have the properties of objects in two domains (for example a 'run time train' that inherits from 'train' and 'graphic icon').

The OOA formalism provides a complete agenda of services to be supported by the architecture.

Much of system development today is performed without any formal notion of architecture. Each individual designer uses his or her own understanding of what is required and then individually creates a design to implement it. Each component is lovingly hand-crafted. The resulting system has two undesirable qualities:

1. The components do not fit together properly, giving rise to the need for a software integration phase.

2. Each component has a different internal structure, making the system harder to understand and therefore more costly to maintain.

A number of projects are currently using the ideas of domain analysis and software architectures, with significant success.

An important point here is that an architecture, like any other domain can also be re-used.

CASE TOOLS FOR MODERN DEVELOPMENT TECHNIQUES

Based on the ideas outlined above, we are in a position to outline a set of top level goals for modern CASE products.

Intelligent support for a rigorous system development method

•   Support for all aspects of the notation. This means supporting not just those parts which are relatively easy to deal with, but also the complex, detailed parts of analysis and design models. For example, in OOA the method requires the analyst to specify in great detail the processing to be carried out by the system in response to events. This processing must be specified with reference to the information model, since this defines all the data that the processing can act on. A competent tool should therefore accept and understand a detailed process model to assist the analyst and check the consistency of the specified processing with the Information Model. It is not acceptable, as many products do, to simply allow free format text input at the most detailed level such that the tool does not, at any stage, 'under stand' the meaning of the information.

- Enforcement of notational rules. A disciplined method includes rules that must be followed for a model to be rigorous and self-consistent. For example in OOA information modelling, a 'subtype' object cannot be related to a 'supertype' object more than once through the same supertype/subtype relationship. Any OOA support tool should therefore prevent the analyst from making such a mistake.

- Automatic addition of model elements where dictated by the method. For example, in OOA information modelling, the formalism requires relationships to be formalised by referential attributes (foreign keys in database terminology). A tool that keeps track of the identifying attributes of objects should be capable of automatically inserting and maintaining the appropriate referential attributes.

- A clear distinction between the underlying information that describes a model and the various possible ways that that information may be viewed. By maintaining a knowledge of this underlying information a tool should be in a position to propagate changes of this information to all the different possible views. The only limit to this idea will be that many views are graphical in nature, and so require extra information related to graphical position and orientation. However, this can either be supplied explicitly by the analyst when he first accesses the view, or can be generated by the tool using layout algorithms.

  An application of this philosophy in OOA would be in inter-object dynamic modelling. The transmission of an event from one object to an other can be viewed both in the processing specification for the transmitting object and on the Object Communication Model (OCM). (The OCM is an overview model which shows the asynchronous communication between all the objects in a domain. An example is shown in Figure 5). Different analysts will wish to adopt different approaches to model building. For some their preferred style will be to sketch out the overall flow of control at the OCM level by identifying asynchronous operations to be provided by objects (event received) and which objects invoke these operations. Others will wish to start with the most detailed levels and have the OCM produced automatically. In either case, we would wish the tool to keep the two views consistent, and propagate facts from one view to another.

- At the simplest level, most notations have conventions for diagram layout, or simply look neater and more readable with particular lay-

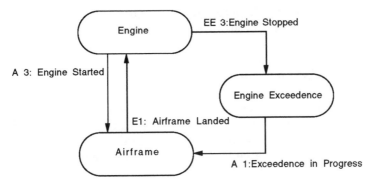

Figure 5   Example fragment of An Object Communication Model

outs. With existing products a considerable period of time is often spent just making the diagram look neat. This is clearly a waste of an analyst's expensive labour. With suitable layout algorithms, a CASE tool should be able to do a major part of this work itself.

One Fact in One Place

A fundamental goal of any tool should be to require the analyst to express the same idea only once. This idea, while simple, has many consequences:

- At the simple level, this means that names of model items should be expressed only once. Whenever the analyst needs to refer to that name, he should be able to do so by picking the item from a list. For example, in OOA, the name of an object is likely to appear in many places such as:

  - On the object in the information model
  - As the name of a data store on a data flow diagram
  - As part of an attribute label on a data flow diagram
  - On the state transition diagram for an object
  - At the head of the object's description

- At a more subtle level, the same idea may be expressed in a number of ways. For example, the notion that an object has dynamic behaviour has the implication not only that it has a state model, but also that it must have an attribute that retains its current status.

Realistic Support for Group Working

The multiuser model whereby analysts work in a single version or copy of a model, by 'checking out' a diagram or database item, modifying it and replacing it is sufficient only for small, close knit teams.

Often, however, on large projects with a significant number of developers, more complex interactions must come into play.

For example, an individual analyst may not have the authority to change certain components of a model. However, he may wish those components to be changed in order to achieve some purpose in an area where he does have authority. Conventional tools allow limited possibilities for resolving this situation:

- Many tools do not support access control that would prevent the analyst from making the unauthorised change.

- Where access control is supported, the analyst will have to ask for the change to be made by a procedure outside, and unsupported by the tool. Since a change may well be complex, this can involve considerable effort.

A better solution would be that the analyst can propose the change from within the tool, by actually making the change to the view that he sees. He can then carry on developing his area of the model, and see the implications of his change. Other analysts would not, however, see the change until it had been approved by the analyst (or reviewer) who does have the authority to make the change.

Seamless Life-Cycle Support

As we have discussed, a fundamental aim of development methods is to specify systems with sufficient rigour at one stage of development, so as to make the progression to the next stage as straightforward as possible. In the context of Recursive Development this can be expressed by considering the diagram shown in Figure 6.

In the process of developing systems using a development method, we typically understand the subject matter, using some formalism (analysis)

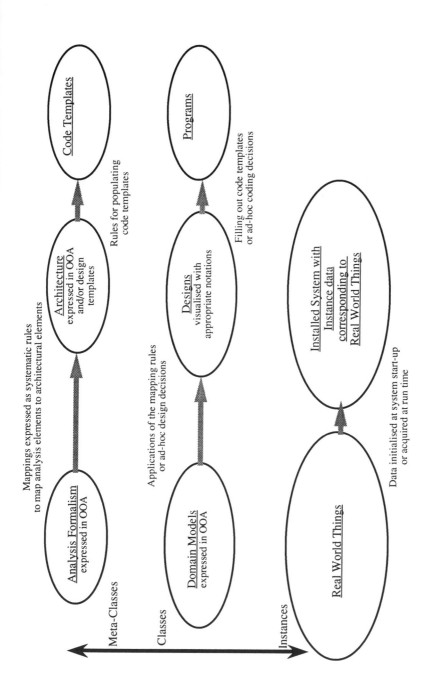

Figure 6 Conceptual Framework of Recursive Design

and subsequently produce a system design based on that analysis. The picture above, generalises this idea as follows:

- Looking at the lowest row of of Figure 6, in building a system we are seeking to map from an understanding of <u>Real World Things</u> to an <u>Installed System</u>. We achieve this activity by:

- Making models of the various subject areas in the problem (<u>Domain Models</u>) and turning these domain models into <u>Designs</u>. The designs must then be turned into code in the shape of <u>Programs</u>. Conventional development methods involve performing this transformation on a domain-by-domain, or even component-by-component basis. Recursive development suggests that we:

- Understand the <u>Analysis Formalism</u> that has been used to express the domain models. Based on an understanding of the <u>Architecture</u> that we wish to use, we evolve a set of systematic rules for trans-forming any domain model expressed in the formalism into a design that conforms to the chosen architecture. Similarly, rather than hand code each design element, we can evolve a set of tem-plates that define rules for coding any design based on the architec-ture. The process of transforming domain models into designs then becomes one of the following rules defined above.

These ideas are very similar to the ideas of computer languages. When called upon to generate machine code from a high level language pro-gram to produce a tabulation of a projectile path, the compiler does not have to understand how to translate the physics of projectiles into code. Rather the compiler must only understand how to translate elements of the high level language into code.

If applied rigorously, this method allows the possibility that a CASE tool that understands the architectures and the mapping rules can apply the rules itself, and thus generate the design and code for a system.

This has a major impact on re-use. Not only is there the possibility that we may re-use the code from domains within other applications, but we may also re-use the analysis/specification in the shape of an OOA model and generate the code for a completely different architecture and target language. This offers much more powerful possibilities than simply using a class browser to pick out a few C++ classes.

THE DEVELOPMENT OF *Intelligent* OOA

Having established the outline goals for a new case tool to support

OOA/RD, we set out to develop one. To do this, we of course chose to use the OOA/RD method itself. This was chosen since we wished to develop a serious high quality product and because it would be a critical test of the method itself.

Figure 7 shows the domain chart for the first release of *Intelligent* OOA.

As can be seen, the issues of method support (OOA and RD) have been abstracted as separate problem areas within the tool. These domains make use of the representational domains to allow the analysts to interact with the models being developed. This achieves one of the fundamental goals of separating the model from its representation.

All the higher level domains were analysed using the OOA formalism.

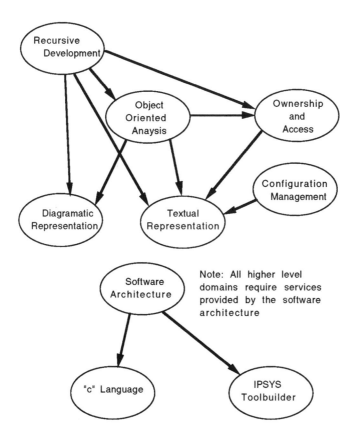

Figure 7   The Domain Chart for *Intelligent* OOA

This has enabled the development of a product that provides a sophisticated level of support.

In summary the domains provide the following services:

- *Recursive Development*
  Allows the creation and manipulation of projects and domains and the use of domains within the projects.

- *Object Oriented Analysis*
  Provides intelligent support for an analyst in building a complete and consistent OOA model. It is here that all the OOA method rules are formalised and used to aid the analyst as information is entered and checks are provided that can detail where information is still to be provided. This domain also achieves the goal of only requiring the analyst to express an idea once. If the analyst makes a change by interacting with either a textual or graphical representation of the model, this domain will automatically calculate and propagate all the consequences of the change, both within the method domain and also by propagating events to all the representations of the model.

- *Ownership and Access*
  As the first step towards providing sophisticated support for team working, this domain provides built in access control and logging mechanisms as well as conventional multiuser access control.

- *Configuration Management*
  Since RD addresses the problem of software reuse as part of the method, *Intelligent* OOA provides a built in configuration management model to enable managers to keep control of the development process. Domains and projects can be baselined, and access to them strictly controlled to prevent, for example, modifications to models that are the subject of external reviews.

- *Diagrammatic and Textual Representations*
  These domains provide the notational representations familiar to users of the method. Typically these domains receive notification from the method domains that a model element has been added, and will work out all the representational consequences of this fact.

- *Software Architecture*
  The analysis of all the higher level domains was performed using OOA. This domain supplies an OOA compliant software architecture. This architecture is synchronous and single threaded with the

provision of an external event queue. This was built on top of the implementation domain detailed below.

- *IPSYS Toolbuilder*
  A key part of the development strategy was to make as much use as possible of existing technology by making use of an existing meta-CASE product. The IPSYS Toolbuilder/TBK product was chosen and provides the low level graphical and textual capabilities as well as the processing base on which the OOA architecture is built. This also provided the functionality to store the instance data in the form of a multiuser, Portable Common Tool Environment-compliant database.

- *'C' Language*
  Although the processing in the high level domains was implemented by use of the Toolbuilder language 'EASEL', the OOA architectural services (event transmission and state machine management) were coded directly in 'C' for greater run time efficiency.

The result of this has been the creation of a product that:

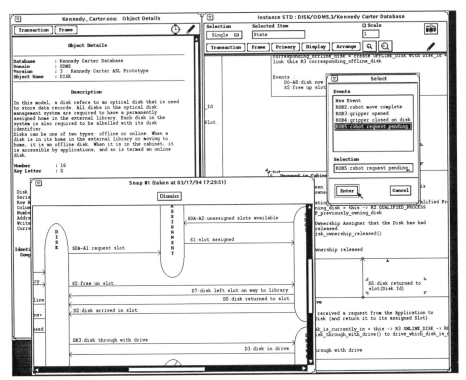

Figure 8   Screen shot of *Intelligent* OOA in use

- Supports the OOA/RD method.

- Allows the analyst to interact with the models in almost any representation and automatically updates all the other views.

- Requires the analyst to enter a fact only once. This is achieved by use of propagation of information and context sensitive pick-lists.

- Prevents the analyst from entering inconsistent information.

- Allows the analyst to enter information however incomplete, in any order, and return later to fill in the gaps.

- Provides support teams of users working on a system, with management control of the development process.

The result has been the efficient creation of high quality models by analysts. The comment most often heard from users is that 'it does just exactly what you would expect that it should do'.

Figure 8 shows a screen shot of the tool in use showing an analyst interacting with a state model (represented by a state transition diagram) with the OCM for the model being kept automatically up to date by the tool.

A recent development has been the definition of an Action Specification Language (ASL) for specification of the processing to be performed in a state.   This is a very high level language providing analysts with the ability to define processing at the OOA level of abstraction, in the standard OOA style. This allows analysts to concentrate on the problem under study without being concerned with exactly how the functions will be implemented in software. ASL provides a number of primitives for:

- Object instance creation and deletion

- Access to attribute values

- Relationship manipulation

- Asynchronous communication between objects (event transmission)

- Services provided by other domains via RD 'bridges'

Since ASL code is defined in the context of an OOA model, the information that it acts upon (object attributes and relationships) is well defined in terms of type and multiplicity. This allows strong type checking to be applied to the ASL code that will help the analyst in ensuring that the processing is not inconsistent with the models that he has already built.

This is an important step since it allows consistent models to be built, even down to the lowest levels of detail. For example, if we wish to obtain a handle on an object that is related to us, for example:

my_dog = this -> 'owns'

might achieve this. The line shown uses a relationship between the object we are working from (an 'owner', specifically 'this') and a related object (the relationship being 'owns'). If, however, we had indicated on the OOA information model that an owner can own several dogs then the ASL statement would be invalid. This is an error that can be checked at compile time, and might prompt the analyst into reassessing his understanding of 'ownership' in the context of this domain. Of course, facilities such as these are already available for information system tools. With OOA/RD, however, the actual implementation could be a commercial relational database system, linked lists in memory or even static arrays.

A code generator has been developed which translates entire OOA models and associated ASL into ANSI 'C'. Together with a host system run time environment, this provides analysts with the ability to simulate, test and debug analysis models at the level of the OOA formalism. This brings a significant set of benefits:

- Analysis models can be rigorously tested out before the target system is ready, and independently of the development of the target architecture.

- A suitable run time architecture for the system can be developed in the knowledge that all the code for the system can be generated automatically. In addition the architectural development work can be performed by the most competent system designers in an organisation without them being distracted by application oriented problems.

- The resulting systems are more easily maintained, since this can be carried out predominantly at the analysis level.

The current version, under beta test on a safety related real time embedded application provides a single task, single threaded asynchronous architecture. Recent work on this has involved studying the possibility of sacrificing some flexibility at run time in order to achieve an extremely fast, low memory usage architecture. This has arisen from the demands of a real time embedded system with very limited processing power and memory available. The necessary work can be achieved without the analysts who developed the domain models being aware of the change in architecture.

CONCLUSION

By examining the lessons of the past we have developed a CASE tool that provides intelligent support for a rigorous and precise system development method (OOA/RD). The tool is being used on a number of large projects world-wide and has been well received by users.

Our work shows that modern development methods, coupled with a serious consideration of the aims of CASE tools can lead to products with great potential. Far from being dead, CASE now offers some very exciting possibilities for the future.

REFERENCES

Carter C B and Raistrick C H. OOA and Recursive Development - A formalism for understanding Software Architectures. *Proceedings of SD92 Conference*, 1992.

Davenport S. CASE Tools - Who Needs Them?, *Software Management*, April 1992, 20.

DeMarco T. *Structured Analysis and System Specification*. Prentice-Hall, 1978.

Jones P. Is CASE at Crisis Point? *Infomatics*, March 1992, 29-34.

Page-Jones M. *The Practical Guide to Structured System Design*. Prentice-Hall, 1980.

Shlaer S and Mellor S J. *Object-Oriented Systems Analysis - Modelling the World in Data*. Prentice-Hall, 1988.

Shlaer S and Mellor S J. Recursive Design, *Computer Language*, 1990.

Shlaer S and Mellor S J. *Object Lifecycles - Modelling the World in States*. Prentice-Hall, 1992.

Sutcliffe A. *Jackson System Development*. Prentice Hall, 1988.

Ward P T and Mellor S J. *Structured Development for Real-Time Systems*. Yourdon, 1985/86.

4

Re-use in Object-Oriented Analysis: An Approach Using Common Fragments

Tim Boreham

ABSTRACT

The object-oriented approach has been suggested as leading towards significant re-use of programming source code. Indications are that this re-use does in fact happen. However, relatively little attention has been given to re-use at a higher level, namely in the abstractions used to develop the Object-Oriented Analysis model. Some earlier work has introduced some standard model fragments; this paper suggests that much of the typical object-oriented analysis model can be made up of these and other standard fragments.

For example, a human resources system deals primarily with people and positions. A suggested fragment for people can be combined with a suggested fragment for organisational structure to give a model relating people to positions. A further feature of many systems is the requirement to deal with time, including past history, and one (or more) proposed

Business Objects: Software Solutions. Edited by Kathy Spurr, Paul Layzell, Leslie Jennison and Neil Richards
© 1994 John Wiley & Sons Ltd

futures. A standard mechanism for dealing with time can be readily introduced. Another typical requirement is that there is a set of rules which specify how the objects under analysis may be associated with one another. A suggested approach for handling general rules and permissions can be added to the model.

Through this approach of combining (more or less) standard fragments, it is expected that a level of increased productivity can be brought to the analysis phase, similar in impact and effect to the increased productivity that occurs through re-use in the programming phase. Some implications for using CASE technology are noted.

INTRODUCTION

In this paper, we discuss the role of re-use in Object Oriented Analysis. Much has been written about re-use at the later stages of the object oriented approach, particularly at the programming stage, but while some attempts have been made to introduce re-use at the earlier stages, this has not gained a widespread following. This paper attempts to address this issue through the introduction of an approach using common fragments. In this approach, we identify a number of common fragments, and show how these can be combined to produce a model which provides most of the features of a full-fledged system.

This approach has arisen through the author's work, and is in constant use. It is intended to be highly practical—in other words, an approach that any practitioner can pick up and use without further study—using their own fragments, or fragments suggested in this and other papers (e.g. Coad, 1992). In fact, it is the author's belief that most experienced practitioners use an approach similar to that described in this paper, although probably with different base concepts and different fragments. It is assumed that readers are familiar with object oriented analysis and the object oriented approach, at least to a base level (there are some good books on the subject, such as Coad, 1991, Rumbaugh, 1991, and others).

The approach at first identifies some common concepts—essentially building block concepts—that can be applied to a wide variety of situations. These building blocks can then be developed into fragments, which are specific to an area. The fragments can then be combined to form actual models, which can be used to develop a system.

For example, the concept of the role played by a person is a building block concept. When we apply this concept to persons occupying positions, we have a fragment. When we combine this fragment with a fragment for organisations, we have a larger fragment that combines persons, positions, and organisations. We introduce a building block concept for capturing history, and we have the beginnings of a human resources system.

The remainder of this paper describes some building blocks, develops them into fragments, and shows how to combine the fragments into a system. Finally, the paper discusses the role of CASE tools in managing and combining the fragments.

BUILDING BLOCK CONCEPTS

The key building block concepts that we will discuss in this section are:

- recursive associations

- history

- roles

- layers and business rules

This section describes these concepts, and shows how they can be applied to, or, in other words, re-used in, a number of situations.

The Recursive Association

This concept is an extremely simple, yet extremely powerful concept. The basic recursive association is shown in Figure 1. This figure shows an Object Class connected to itself through the recursive association is-comprised-of. The meaning of this recursive association is that each object instance in the class can be comprised of a number of other object

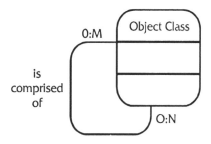

Figure 1   Recursive Association

instances, and equally, each object instance may form part of other object instances. Since this cannot continue in either direction forever, some object instances will be at the top, and form part of no other instances; equally, some instances will at the bottom, and will be indivisible units.

This building block can be applied in a number of situations. Let us take three as examples:

- Organisations

- Materials

- Holdings

Once we have seen how this process works with organisations, the translation to materials and holdings is trivial.

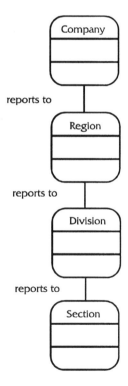

Figure 2   Organisational Hierarchy

An Example: Organisations

Typically, an organisation, such as a government department, or a company, is organised along the lines shown in Figure 2.

This structure accurately models the current real world. However, as always, things change. The result is typically that additional classes need to be introduced, as, for example, with the introduction of a *Department* between the *Division* and the *Region*. The use of the recursive association eliminates these problems.

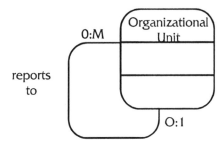

Figure 3   Organisational Unit

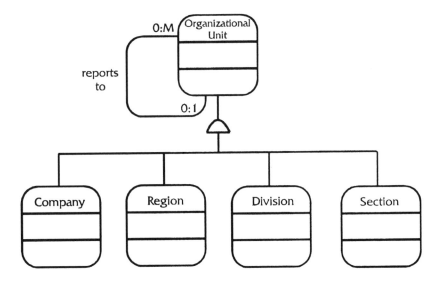

Figure 4   Adding Inheritance

Now, the addition of extra levels in the organisational hierarchy has no impact on the model, and, correspondingly, and perhaps more importantly, no impact on the resulting system. However, it may be that each of the different types of organisational unit has different characteristics (attributes and/or methods). In this case, we can readily add these different types as sub-classes of the major class, Organisational Unit.

It is worth noting the differences between this model and the earlier model (Figure 2). First, we can introduce new classes (such as *Department*) with only a minor impact on the model. Secondly, the users have complete flexibility, at least at the model level, as to how the structure is arranged. For example, should an exception occur, such as a section reporting directly to a region, the model is unaffected. However, if it is necessary to prevent this occurring, it can be accomplished through the addition of business rules, and these are much easier to change than the model structure.

A very similar process can be applied to materials. In a manufacturing environment, this type of recursive association is extremely common. However, it is often applicable anywhere that materials are used. For example, in the construction of houses, we could use a similar structure to describe a house and its components. In a warehouse, we can use a similar structure to show the goods that are being handled (note that in many warehousing systems, it is possible for a stock item to be made up of other stock items).

Similarly, this association can also be applied to more conceptual matters. For example, if we take a person's (or a company's) holdings at a bank, we can see that their holdings may be made up of a number of different types, such as bank accounts and investments. Each of these may be further broken down into different types: accounts into savings and chequing, and investments into fixed income and equities. It is important to note that while the inheritance model may have these levels, the recursive association allows us to position any holding as a component of any other holding. For example, we may decide to have the class *fixed income investments* inherit from *investments*, because its attributes and methods more closely correspond to that of *investments*. However, the client tells us that they consider *fixed income investments* as part of their bank accounts, and want them structured that way. This gives us the class diagram as in Figure 5, while the actual objects are arranged as in Figure 6 (Figure 6 is an object occurrence diagram showing individual object occurrences, not classes).

History

History can be handled in a deceptively simple manner. Typically, a

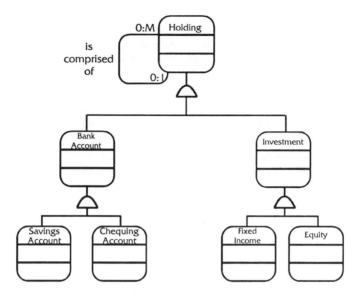

Figure 5   Holdings Object Classes

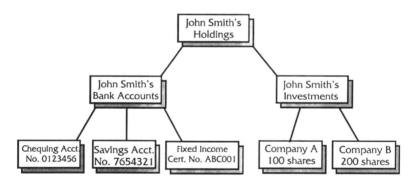

Figure 6   John Smith's Holdings (Object Instances)

model is built, and it turns out that, rather than representing a point in time, the client wants us to keep history in the model. This can be accomplished by simply adding two attributes, *start_date* and *end_date* to each applicable class, and a method that checks whether a supplied date is between the *start_date* and the *end_date*. This simple practice leads to some significant benefits.

First, it enables us to record multiple objects of each class, with differing start and end dates. For example, if we record the *position* that each *person* fills in our organisation, an object class assignment with the attributes *start_date* and *end_date*, together with associations to person and *position* nicely records all of the *positions* that a *person* has held (Figure 7).

In addition to recording the history, this approach also allows us to specify a particular date, and have the objects respond only if that date is between their *start_date* and *end_date*. Now we can see the situation at any point in time. Further, the date specified could be in the future, allowing us to see the behaviour of the system in a situation that has not yet come to pass. This can, of course, be used for testing possible scenarios.

In addition, any objects which are present in the system *automatically* activate when the current date passes their start date. In other words, by putting the changes into the system in advance, the system automatically takes on its new configuration when a supplied date passes the *start_date* and/or *end_date* of an object.

There are a few points to note about this:

- It is sometimes suggested that only a single date be held in an object, and it be automatically superseded when a new object is created with a later *start_date*. While it is true that the information is duplicated, and therefore steps must be taken to synchronise the *end_date* of the previous object with the *start_date* of the next, it is much easier to implement if each object has sufficient information to be able to make a decision as to whether is should be active without consulting other objects in its class. There are those who will say that this is a physical consideration, and should be omitted from the Analysis; to them I can only say 'guilty', and that it is included because it helps understand how the system will work.

- The simplest way to establish a particular point in time is by means of a *Date_server* object. The *Date_server* simply returns, on request, the effective date for the current activity. In a simple system, the

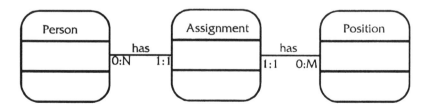

Figure 7   Person is Assigned to Position

Date_server may just store the date, but, in most practical implementations, it looks up the desired date based on the user or process id.

- A decision must be made as to the way in which objects which have no currently determined *end_date* are represented. The simplest solution is to have them hold a date which is beyond that envisaged for the system, such as 2099 December 31. Unfortunately, this invariably leads to a problem, as a user tries to determine what the system would look like in 2100 January 1! Perhaps it would be possible to pick a suitable date, but in my experience, any such date is doomed to (eventual) failure. It is therefore suggested that a *not_a_date* value be chosen—in some systems, this could be NULL. This does involve an extra check, but it can also save a lot of difficulty.

Roles

A role describes the characteristics that an object may take on in the system, while remaining an object of its underlying class. For example, a procurement system may include a *supplier* class. In fact, the underlying object is, perhaps, *legal_entity*, where a *legal_entity* may be either a *person* or a *company*. *Supplier* is, in fact, a role they play with regards to the company building the system. With regards to other companies, they are *customers*, and frequently they are customers of the companies to which they are suppliers.

It seems that this situation is best handled through *roles* (see, for example, Coad, 1992). In this case, there would be both *supplier* and *customer* classes. These classes behave exactly like the usual *supplier* and *customer* classes, except that, rather than embedding in the class the information about the underlying object, there is instead an association with that underlying object. This allows any underlying object to play as many roles as necessary. The concept is shown in Figure 8.

This building block concept allows us to treat the underlying objects as if they were *suppliers* or *customers*, as the case may be, while preserving the unity of the underlying object. Thus, for example, if there were a change of address for the company, the change would take place in the underlying object, rather than in the *customer* or *supplier* object. This ensures that the information is common across the roles.

Layers and Business Rules

It often seems helpful to think of the model under development as having *layers*. In a typical situation, we can consider the following layers:

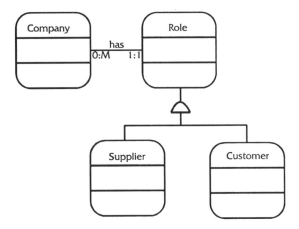

Figure 8   Roles

1.   The base layer describes the actual situation; in other words, it holds the objects corresponding to the real world, with the base information and behaviour corresponding to the real world. As an example, this layer may contain an object representing, say, John Smith, an object representing a position, say, Director of Finance, and an object representing the connection between them (the fact that John Smith is currently Director of Finance). This layer does not contain anything about whether or not John Smith is qualified to be Director of Finance—it simply contains the actual situation.

2.   The next layer can be considered the *layer of the possible*. This layer describes the possible configurations of the bottom layer—specifying, for example, the qualifications required to be Director of Finance. In most cases this layer forms part of the resulting system, which allows the users to change the business rules, if required.

3.   The third layer is only required when the users are allowed to change the business rules in the second layer. This third layer describes the possible (allowable) business rules—in other words, it may require every position to have qualifications that are suitable for the position. This layer therefore contains the rules about rules, or metarules, and can be called the metarule layer. For example, the metarule layer may contain a rule that says that any finance position must require, among the qualifications, either experience, a diploma, or a degree in finance. The specific rules required can be created by the user, as long as they meet this restriction.

Figure 9 illustrates these layers.

In practice, in the analysis stage, these layers can be handled in several different ways. Probably the most common way is to combine the layers, and let each object make its own decision about what is allowed. This approach works well in simple situations, but in more complex areas can lead to some difficulty, because the objects can become too complex. Another way is to directly model the business rules layer by adding a layer of objects (one per class in the base layer), which contain the business rules applicable to the corresponding base layer objects. Then, each base layer object can ask the corresponding shadow object for its class as to whether each particular change is allowable. In some cases, this additional set of objects can work quite successfully, but in highly complex situations, another approach seems to be more successful. The complexity of the interface, and often, of the rule layer, can be reduced by introducing a *rule_server* (see, for example Hilton *et al.*, 1993). The *rule_server* encapsulates the rule layer, separating the structure of that layer from the structure of the layer that it serves. This means that the rules can be expressed in many forms—either as a rule-based expert system, for example, with generalised rules, or as a cooperating collection of objects, or a combination of the two, as is commonly found in current expert systems shells.

Note that some simple rules, such as a rule in a human resources system that every organisational unit must have at least one position, can

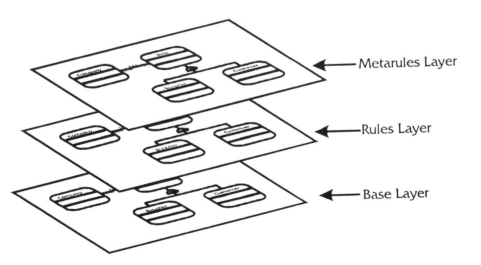

Figure 9   Layers

be handled in the usual way, by adding cardinalities (1:M) to the association. It is only more complex rules that need a more complex mechanism to enforce them.

The effect of this separation between the layers is to ensure that the base layer objects only 'worry' about what *is*, not what *could be*. This significantly simplifies the task of these objects. Any question as to whether a change is valid is handled by a separate object, either a corresponding object in the business rules layer, or a rule server.

DEVELOPING FRAGMENTS

Based on our building block concepts above, we can now begin to develop *fragments* which apply these concepts to specific areas. For the purposes of this paper, three areas are suggested:

*   A human resources system

*   A warehousing system

*   A manufacturing system.

In this section, we will develop the fragments, and apply them to the specified areas.

Human Resources

In this system, the human resources department of a corporation wants information to manage the human resources. For the purposes of this paper, we will restrict ourselves to the issues of the organisational units, and the people that fill the positions in those units. We also want to maintain the addresses of the units and the people, and the telephone numbers (voice, fax) of the people.

First, we identify the key base level object classes involved:

*   Person

*   Organisational Unit

*   Position

*   Address (location)

*   Telephone Number

We proceed by applying our building block concepts to the area. For example, we can identify the organisational structure as a recursive association. We can identify the recursive association *reports to* between positions. We can also identify address as a recursive association of *locations* (an apartment number in a building on a street in a city; for those who think that this introduces unnecessary complexity, bear in mind that the *implementation* of the address could reduce to the traditional four or five lines of text).

We can then introduce associations:

- A person *holds* a position

- A position *reports to* a position

- A position *is in* an organisational unit

- A person, a position and an organisational unit may *have* location(s)

- A person, a position, an organisational unit, and, possibly, an address may *have* telephone number(s) (possibly of different types).

This leads us to the diagram shown in Figure 10.

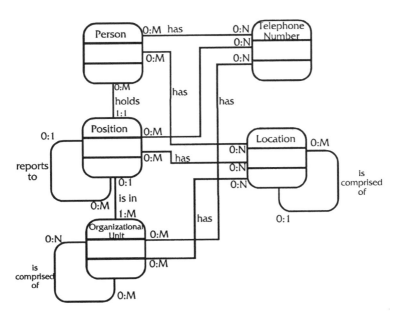

Figure 10   Human Resources Fragment

We can now introduce the concept of history, by adding *start_date* and *end_date* to each of the objects, and by also adding these attributes to new objects introduced to handle the associations. The result of applying two simple building block concepts is a model that can provide a significant amount of the base information necessary for a human resources function, with only five object classes (excluding the object classes derived from the associations).

Obviously, significant complexity must yet be added to this model to make it function appropriately as a human resources system. However, the bulk of the complexity can be added in two ways:

- First, through adding subclasses to the existing classes; and

- Second, by adding separate classes (perhaps a rule server) to handle the rules.

Effectively, our building block concepts have allowed us to develop a fragment that can be used as the core of a human resources system, with a significant amount of flexibility, and with only five classes (excluding classes derived from the associations). This fragment is deceptively simple, but, by placing the rules in separate objects, and allowing the complexity of different subtypes to be handled by inheritance, we have a fragment which can handle many, perhaps even most, of the activities and information of the complete system.

Additionally, this fragment is applicable for any system which needs to know about persons, positions, organisational units, addresses, and telephone numbers, such as:

- A supplier, or customer, management system

- An equipment maintenance system

- A manufacturing system, or

- A warehousing system.

Of course, in each case the orientation of the system is different, and people, positions, and units often play a smaller role than in a human resources system, but the core fragment remains the same.

Warehousing System

In this example, we consider a system which is responsible for moving stock items into locations within a warehouse, and moving them out on request. Sometimes, a collection of stock items may form a unit, which must be shipped in its entirety, or not at all. These stock items may be of different sizes, and may be stored in locations according to their sizes.

We can identify three major base classes:

- A stock item

- A location

- A transport mechanism (object).

This last object class, transport mechanism, represents all of the various means by which a stock item may be moved—ranging from a conveyor belt to a fork-lift truck, and perhaps even a person.

We can immediately use our recursive association on *stock item, location* and, possibly, on *transport mechanism*. This last depends upon details of the transport system which have not been stated above, such as whether the warehouse is automated, partially automated or manual. Note that we can simplify the system by considering the shipping and receiving areas as locations, perhaps with unlimited capacity. Additionally, we can identify the following association:

- A stock item *is moved to* a location by a transport mechanism.

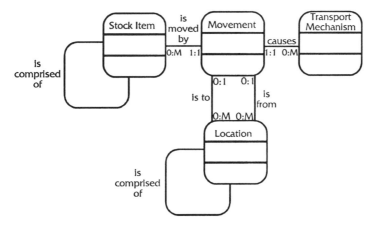

Figure 11   Warehouse Fragment

We can now add an object class to represent the *is_moved_to* association, which leads us to the diagram in Figure 11.

By adding history to the *is_moved_to* class, we can handle much of the information requests a system of this type must answer. A question like 'where is <item>' can be handled by simply finding the current instance of the *is_moved_to* object class for that item. Movement requests can be entered by adding future instances of the *is_moved_to* class, and the transport objects can develop a pick list by collecting together these instances and selecting and ordering them.

Note that neither of the object classes stock item or transport must participate in the association with the *is_moved_to* objects. This means that a stock item can be moved without having to reference a transport—this is typically useful for stock items arriving at receiving, or leaving from shipping. Equally, a transport object can be moved without necessarily moving a stock item—this enables us to determine where our transport objects are at all times (assuming they notify the system!).

This model can handle much, perhaps most, of the activities and information associated with a warehousing system. Again, the use of our building blocks, together with placing some of the complexity in a rule layer (or rule server), and using inheritance to represent sub-classes, provides us with a simple, flexible, yet powerful model.

This fragment can be used to represent stock items and locations in a variety of systems, such as a retail store stocking system, in addition to its use in a warehousing system.

Manufacturing System

In this case, we consider a situation where various parts and materials go through a process, involving machines and people, which result in them becoming finished product. The type of product they become may vary, and the processes depend on the type of product. In some cases, the machines may need to be programmed to carry out the specified process; this program must be supplied to the machine before the process can start.

We can identify the following key object classes:

- Work-in-progress

- Product

- Process

- Resource.

We can apply our recursive association immediately to *work_in_progress*, to *product*, to *process* and to *resource*. While we need not expand the hierarchy at this time, we can see that a *resource* must include both machines and human resources.

It is not intended that a single *work_in_process* object handle all the work in process, but that, rather, any groupings of objects are handled by this object class. For example, there may be a grouping of objects which are intended to become part of the same finished good, or there may be a grouping of objects which will be processed together (a batch). The system is simplified considerably if both raw materials (incoming parts) and finished goods are considered different stages of *work_in_process*.

Note that in a manufacturing system, by its very nature, a *work_in_process* object changes characteristics significantly between its creation and it becoming a finished good (or a part of one). Frequently, there are processes in which multiple *work_in_process* objects entering the process emerge as (components of) a single, new, *work_in_process* object. Equally, depending upon the specific system being modelled, there may be processes in which a single *work_in_process* object entering the process emerges as multiple, new *work_in_process* objects. Both of these situations are handled by the recursive association for *work_in_process*.

We can identify the following associations:

- Work-in-progress *becomes* (*is_to_become*) product

- A resource *works_on* work_in_process using a process.

We can also identify some associations in the rule layer:

- Product *requires* process

- Process *may use* resource.

In this latter case, the association identifies which specific resource instances are associated with (are allowed to use) which specific process objects. There may be a further layer which determines which objects are allowed to be associated in this way by, for example, machine type or operator qualifications, or some combination.

If we draw the base level associations, and expand the *works_on* association into an object class called *work*, we get the diagram shown in Figure 12.

By adding history to the *work* object, we can see that this diagram, as with the others, satisfies much of the base needs of the manufacturing system. We can ask a *work_in_process* object what product it is supposed

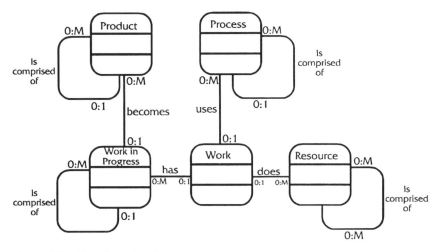

Figure 12   Manufacturing Fragment

to become, and what processes have been carried out on it. We can identify how much use has been made of a resource, and, because we allow a *work* object not to involve a *work_in_process* object, we can allow for maintenance to be carried out on a resource.

By adding a rule server, we can have the *work_in_process* object ask the rule server what process should be carried out on it next, and then ask the rule server what resources should be assigned to carry out that process. The rule server can use the information described above in the rule layer, and the information in the base layer, to determine the next resource to be used. If one of the resources is a transport system, we can have the *work_in_process* object request transport to its next location (the process is 'move me to <location>').

Again, through the use of our building block concepts, we have developed a simple model that can handle much of the requirements of a manufacturing system. This is a fairly broad class of system, yet our fragment can be relatively easily adapted to support these widely differing systems.

USING CASE

In this section we discuss the support that a CASE tool can provide to this process. At the most basic level, the CASE tool can be used as a centralised repository for the fragments, which can then be incorporated into the current model. This, of course, assumes that the CASE tool is multi-user, and has a capability, and the appropriate and necessary controls, to maintain a central repository.

There are two other possible features of CASE tools, under the above assumptions, which would greatly assist this process:

- A capability for a CASE tool to support a template would allow the building block concepts to be stored in a CASE tool, and applied as required. For this capability to work to the organisation's best advantage, there would have to be a basic capability to update the template from the resulting model, if desired. This feature would enable an organisation to develop, expand, and build up a collection of building blocks which could be made available to all the analysts.

- It appears that most CASE tools currently have a capability to store fragments, at worst, as entire models. However, for the organisation to gain the most benefit, it is necessary for the CASE tool to support extracting a revised fragment from a complete model, and adapting that fragment to a more generalised purpose.

CONCLUSION

Benefits

Perhaps the most important benefits of an object oriented analysis approach using building blocks and templates are the same benefits we expect from any reuse: greater productivity, and more standardisation.

The increase in productivity comes about in two ways. First, in the analysis phase, because the analyst can match the situation with building blocks and or fragments, and assemble these quickly into a core model. Second, in the design and construction phases, the resulting model corresponds closely with existing code, either because the analyst used common fragments, which already exist, or because the analyst used building blocks. Object classes in existing systems can be used as patterns to build the new classes.

The increase in standardisation occurs in much the same way. Through re-use of existing fragments, the same problem is solved in the same way in every system. Through re-use of the building block concepts, new fragments are developed which match existing fragments in style and approach.

Summary

In this paper, we have attempted to show how an approach using building block concepts and fragments can lead to a significant level of re-use during analysis. The building block concepts separate the model into its core components, and move the complexity to inherited object classes and a rule server, or a business rules layer. The results, when applied to a specific application area, are object model fragments which are sufficiently general and flexible to cover a wide variety of situations, while retaining the power necessary to ensure that the fragments provide a saving in the work required.

I am most interested in the experience of those who are already using, or those who intend to use, a similar approach. It would be very useful if these concepts could be collected together and provided as a 'cookbook' of object oriented analysis for the beginning practitioner.

REFERENCES AND BIBLIOGRAPHY

Booch G. *Object Oriented Design with Applications*. Benjamin-Cummings, 1991
Coad P and Yourdon E. *Object-Oriented Analysis: 2nd ed*. Yourdon Press/Prentice Hall, 1991.
Coad P. Object-Oriented Patterns. *ACM Commun*. **35**(9), September 1992, 152-159.
Hilton C, Rice J and Sridharan N. Modeling: The Key to Flexible CIM Software. *Towards World Class Manufacturing Conference Proceedings*, September 1993.
Meyer B. *Object-Oriented Software Construction*. Prentice-Hall, 1988.
Norman D. *The Psychology of Everyday Things*. Basic Books, 1988.
Rumbaugh J, Blaha M, Premerlani W, Eddy F and Lorensen W. *Object-Oriented Modeling and Design*. Prentice-Hall, 1991.

Section 2

*Development Methods
and Tools*

5

OMT Development Process, Vintage 1994

Don Kavanagh

ABSTRACT

The book OMT (*Object Modelling Technique*) by James Rumbaugh *et al.* was published in 1991 (Rumbaugh, 1991). Many projects today are adopting OMT as their OO analysis and design method. This paper reviews and expands on the current techniques of Use Cases and CRC (Class, Responsibility and Collaboration) that enhance the OMT development models, and how the development process is being applied to explore the early development phases of the OMT models. The paper also touches on the use of CASE tools in OO system development.

PROJECT DEVELOPMENT

One of the first key areas of a development project is to understand the modelling techniques and the essential focuses of the development as we move from requirements to code.

Business Objects: Software Solutions. Edited by Kathy Spurr, Paul Layzell, Leslie Jennison and Neil Richards
© 1994 John Wiley & Sons Ltd

Models described in most OO texts are perceived as two dimensional diagrams—flat snap-shots of the completed project, such as the OMT Object Model—but within a project development life-cycle they must take on a third dimension of depth. The models have to be started and enriched as the problem and solution domain of the evolving system is explored and defined.

The OMT book provides an excellent text on the notation and structure of the models, but lacks emphasis on the techniques used to develop and refine the models during the early phases of a project life-cycle.

OVERVIEW OF OMT

OMT system development consists of four different phases that follow each other seamlessly. In the early phase of analysis, a problem oriented specification is developed, i.e. a specification of what the system is to offer the users. At this early stage of system development, when changes are still relatively inexpensive, the aim is to find a flexible structure of the system: a structure that is robust against changes and that gives the system a clear and comprehensible division into objects that provide operations (services). The key element of this specification is called the Object Model. It outlines the basic relationships of objects in the system under ideal circumstances and without regard to a particular implementation environment. In other words, in the analysis model we disregard any restrictions that might exist in the programming language, database management system and other surrounding supporting system products. The evolution of the requirement analysis Object Model is thus focused on the problem domain.

OMT progressively adds detail to the models throughout the development, until in the detailed design stages the class models and structures are turned into code. A key advantage of the OMT method is that it uses the same modelling notation throughout the life-cycle, so there are no abrupt transitions to another notation or semantic interpretation as a separate design stage. OMT provides models of different detailing degrees. The early models are very abstract, focusing on external and domain qualities of the system, whereas the later models become more detailed and solution-oriented in the way in which they describe how the system is going to be built and how it should function.

A technique is an approach to the development of a system, in any of its phases, that is used to create a particular diagram or model. There are many different techniques proposed in OMT that can be applied at different points in the life-cycle. Use cases and CRC are documented techniques from Jacobson, and Wirfs-Brock, respectively, that will be explored in more detail below, as they are useful in providing the focus of attention into the relevant issues of early object modelling.

A system that is based on an object orientated philosophy or modelling consists of a number of objects. By objects, I mean a clearly delimited part of the modelled or designed system, usually corresponding to an entity in real life, e.g. an invoice, a plane or a telephone. Each object has a specified content and holds information meant for that particular object.

All information in an object oriented system is stored in the objects and can only be manipulated if and when the objects are requested to perform operations. The behaviour and representation of its information are encapsulated in the object; they are not visible from outside the object.

The use of an object oriented technique in a development will provide a consistent flow to the development process where the real life-like objects of the analysis phase can be transformed into detailed object design models and subsequently code, with a structure that closely follows that of the analysis model.

OMT MODELS

In the earlier event modelling and structuring, the OMT environment has a rich set of diagrams and models, allowing the concept of a system to be defined. OMT views a system in three key areas:

1. The objects, the things that are of interest to the system.

2. The dynamic behaviour of the system and its constraints on when and how it may respond to different stimuli.

3. The processes and procedures that provide the functionality of the system transformations (Figure 1).

The three key models are:

1. Object Model   —the things of the application

2. Dynamic Model   —the interactions and constraints

3. Functional Model   —the operations, computations and
                           transformations

A model is a collection of diagrams, often partitioning a subset of the method notation, that provides a visualisation of the abstraction of the system domain under consideration, be it analysis, dynamic design, class

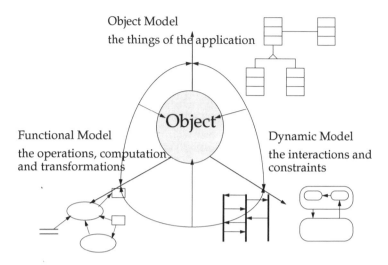

Figure 1   The Three Key Models of OMT

implementation, etc. In the earlier event modelling and structuring, the OMT environment has a rich set of diagrams, allowing the definition of both the concept of a system to be defined with its external actors in the context diagram, and the event flows between the system. Scenarios describe a sequence of events and are visualised in event trace diagrams. The event trace diagram shows classes as vertical bars spaced across the diagram and the events are shown as horizontal arrows between them. The diagram shows a top to bottom time ordering or sequence ordering of events in the scenario modelled.

Finally, the dynamic aspects of the system are summarised in the event flow diagram. It shows classes, and the interaction of all of the events between classes defined in the event trace diagrams. The classes are represented by rectangles, which is similar to the Object Model, but does not show relationships between classes.

The model, combined with the notation, then provides a critical mechanism for managing the complexity of a given viewpoint of abstraction, for a given system. The use of models, and the definition of specific viewpoint diagrams of a class abstraction and closure, then allows a reader to navigate effectively through a large analysis model to the desired expression of a systems requirement. The model allows the reader to gain access to information about particular aspects of a complex system easily.

LIFE-CYCLE AND OMT

At any point in time in a project's development, there is a given set of models, comprising of a range of diagrams and associated text elements. Let us briefly consider how the models are refined through the development process and the typical development phases in OMT (Kavanagh, 1994):

1. Requirements Analysis   —what must be done

2. System Design   —develop system architecture

3. Object Design   —fully define classes and relationships

4. Implementation   —transformation of models into target languages.

Each successive phase in the development adds to the result of the previous step and furthers the development of the system. Thus, both the formalism and degree of the specification of the system increase until the final detailing level is reached—the program code. This provides an incremental but iterative approach to the development.

The OMT Object Model is the foundation of each phase, and it describes the things of the application in application-related concepts (e.g. service). As it forms the basis of the design, the structure of the implementation will mirror the structure of the problem, rather than the other way round. This provides greater consistency through the life-cycle.

ADDING TECHNIQUES TO OMT

Taking the OMT models as the basis of a development, the next step is to explore some of the techniques which have been used in object oriented approaches in the last 2–3 years, and which are now being more commonly applied to OMT to enhance the base process of how we capture system requirements and record them in the OMT notation and models. Why is it necessary to do this? OMT is a very useful notation, as it has very strong diagrams and models within the method for describing the various aspects of the system such as the Object Model, the Dynamic Model, plus a number of associated models, but it lacks guidance early in the OMT development process.

One of the key aspects is being able to take a given set of developers and have them repeat a development and produce a consistent viewpoint, a consistent set of diagrams, notes and problem statements. If they can't do this, while there are many possible solutions to a system, there should be few interpretations of the requirements. It should be reasonable to argue that there is only potentially one problem, as a consensus of those that require the system. Modelling and understanding or communicating that consensus is a key issue. If we can derive six different Object Models from the same potential consensus of the user, it may mean that each one of them has captured some expectation of each of the users. Alternatively, it could be that the expectations of the user have been missed entirely, as the analyst's interpretation of the requirements may not necessarily be what the user perceives as their true need.

A basic requirement of a good method is that it simplifies the development of systems. Thus a good method for object oriented system development should help identify the right objects. This may seem obvious, but many methods for object oriented development actually treat this aspect of development superficially, implying that there is no difficulty finding the objects directly in the activity that is to be modelled.

The OMT book in its initial approach gives us the idea of a process to find the initial objects of a development by picking out the nouns and the verbs in the requirement document or problem statement and then iterating over the Object Model diagrams, making nouns into object/classes and verbs into relationships, in terms of reasoning about what is a good class and what we think would be a relevant relationship. This is predominantly done within the analyst's mind. This process can be difficult and becomes subjective to the analyst who is looking at it. Now while it is valuable to get a basic vocabulary of the problem domain and the users definition and interpretation of requirements, we also need ways to be able to refine and expand and revisit those requirements and make sure that they are being expressed in the true nature of the expectation in which the user wrote them.

A more powerful way is also to utilise and enhance this information and process with the contribution of users and other domain experts, and then being able to reason and capture requirements of the system to refine the object model and the dynamic behaviour associated with it more fully. We need techniques in OMT to allow us to explore the problem domain more fully, and to reach a consensus, not only between the potential users and their expectations of the system, but also to the analysts and ultimately the implementation of the system.

One of the most valuable aspects of human beings is creativity, but it can be difficult to get it started. It can be the old phrase of analysis paralysis—what is the correct starting point. Poorly communicated requirements in the initial problem definition can greatly affect the outcome and the shape of the perceived solution, and often it will have a much greater effect than would have been expected. Misinterpretation of customers words is one of the most common problems of system development today. We pay lawyers large sums of money to interpret and record discussions correctly, so that they are not ultimately misinterpreted in contracts and communication between people. User's software requirement documents are written with far less rigor in mind and far less control of the language used within them. But the document is often the basis of the entire development process.

How often have you agonised over a particular word to try and capture your understanding and your feeling of a particular requirement? Or you are writing a report and are trying to decide how to phrase it and get just the right emphasis. You may reach for the thesaurus, or press a button, to come up with a myriad of alternatives within the English language to allow you to try and express your understanding.

CASE Tools such as Requirements Management and Repository Reuse Browsers are starting to help in capturing or stripping English requirements documents, and allowing sentences and key phrases to be marked. They can then be queried to provide a viewpoint on all the requirements related to some key word. This allows inconsistencies and contradictions to be spotted early. The repository browser of the StP (Software through Pictures) OMT tool by IDE (Interactive Development Environment) allows analysts to quickly search project libraries for domain or application objects that may have been previously specified, reducing the early project work. The re-use of high level objects in projects is still immature, but treating objects as assets is very important. Effective tool support is necessary to quickly find and retrieve items at the point at which they are needed. Class capture utilities also allow StP to populate libraries and project repositories with standard C++ libraries, not defined as part of a previous analysis. This brings tremendous potential for reusing and specialising generic and domain objects early in a project.

The power of thought, if harnessed in a positive and productive manner, to seek a better and more refined presentation, is an amazing tool. We can look, refine and argue, even if we could never have created the potential solution. So to be able to iterate over a proposed OMT model is one of the most powerful tools we can use in any approach to system and software development.

Iterative development is often mentioned in OO projects, but is often not explained. Briefly, iterative development is a scheduling phase strategy, supporting predicted rework of portions of the system. Incremental development is a scheduling and staging strategy, allowing portions of the system to be developed at different times or rates, and integrated as they are completed. These definitions identify incremental and iterative development as independent concepts to be used separately or together. The intention of incremental development is to develop a system piece by piece, and to permit additions to the requirements, improvements to the development process, or changes to the scheduling. The intent of an iterative strategy is to allow correction of mistakes and development improvements based upon user feedback, architectural and performance tuning, or maintenance criteria, and to allow it in a controlled manner. The essential characteristic of incremental development in OMT is that the system is developed in portions based on the objects and phases of the development subsystem. As each object or subsystem is completed, it is added to the growing system definition. There may be a period of evaluation after the integration of one increment and before work on the next increment is begun, to gather feedback and new requirements. Alternatively, the increments may be phased in parallel. In a non-iterative but incremental project, the increments are developed to full production standards from the start. This may be a subsystem that can then be tested and considered for reuse in other systems.

Iterative development is often considered in a negative way, in that iteration is done to correct problems or mistakes that were missed in previous iterations. A more productive view should be taken, as the positive act of discovery. It is natural to go through a refinement process as requirements and potential solution architectures are discovered. The critical element is to limit the scope and semantics of iteration to a clear set of defined phases. This fits naturally into the use case and CRC iterative refinement of a problem more easily than a traditional waterfall life-cycle.

USE CASE AND OMT

One technique that is beginning to be used to enhance OMT is that of *Use Case*. Use cases, as described by Jacobson (1992), is a technique which focuses on the external objects of a given system. The analyst considers the system to be like a 'black box' (Figure 2). The use case becomes an expression of how users would describe the expected interaction between itself and the system in terms of the domain objects they perceive to be important. For any one particular project, there can be many users, each with many uses for the system under development. A user is viewed as an 'actor', and can be human or machine. Each actor may perform a number of tasks, each of which uses the system in some way. When an actor performs a behaviourally related sequence of transactions in a dialogue with the system we call this a use case. Each use case is a

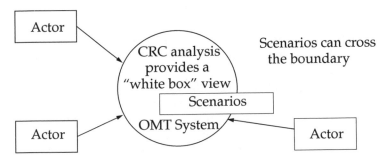

Figure 2   How to View the Pieces: Use Cases Provide a 'Black Box' View.

specific way to use the system, a case of usage. The collection of use cases can become the complete functional requirements of the system to be built. For example, an input clerk may feed sales information into the system, and that is their sole use of the system. Another user may input payroll data, print out payslips, cheques and wage dockets. Each of these uses of the system is a use case. One actor of the system may only perform a single use case, or may perform many, depending upon their view of the system. Each use case is defined by a description. The system should thus be able to perform everything described in all of the use cases defined. Use cases can be a useful reference point running though all activities developing subsequent models, helping to maintain a strong focus on the problem at each point in its evaluation.

To find the use cases within a project, we ask questions like 'What are the main tasks of each actor?', and 'Will the actor have to inform the system about outside changes?' When analysing and describing use cases in detail, it is not unusual for unclear points in the requirement specification to be revealed. Vague requirements thus become obvious at an early stage, allowing refinement to take place.

There is quite a strong relationship between use cases, as proposed by Jacobson, and the scenarios already in use in OMT modelling. The OMT book (Rumbaugh, 1991) describes a scenario as a sequence of events that occurs during one particular execution of a system. The scope of a scenario can vary; it may include all events in the system, or it may include only those events impinging on or generated by certain objects in the system. A scenario can also be the historical record of executing a system, or a thought experiment of executing a proposed system. But there is little guidance as to how to effectively explore scenarios.

The use case can be likened to a class of similar interactions, and the scenario a particular instance of use case. Use cases can be applied very early on with respect to the OMT process to enhance it and provide a more repeatable understanding and representation of the problem domain.

Once a set of use cases has been identified within a project, by choosing a number of critical use cases (between 5 and 10) that can be considered to be the most important features of a system, we can exercise the widest interaction of objects and system behaviour to determine which areas may be at risk, and which are critical features.

Rumbaugh (1993) suggests a number of objects that separate the control and co-ordination of use cases/scenarios from interface behaviour and from domain objects embodying the concepts in the area of the application. By keeping external behaviour, internal structure and dynamics apart, each may be altered or extended independently of the other objects. This also provides a focus as to what are the key objects in each development phase.

The applications objects used in the analysis phase are interface, format and control objects. Each type of object has a different purpose. A persistent entity object models information in the system that should be held for some period of time, typically surviving a use case. All behaviour naturally and closely coupled to this information is placed within the domain object. Domain objects usually correspond to something in the real world, outside the system, although this is not always the case. The application object models behaviour and information that is dependent on the actual interface of the system. The task of an interface object is to translate the actor's actions with the system into events in the system, and to translate those events in the system that the actor is interested in into something presented to the actor, via display objects.

Use cases, when used as an enhancement to OMT, may form the basis of system acceptance testing. They may also be used to quickly refine the first cut OMT Object Model, validating key objects and classes, taking the use cases forward to become specific scenarios to be used in the second OMT enhancement technique, CRC.

Use cases and OMT can have multiple benefits of:

• refining the understanding of the critical use case/scenario chosen

• stimulating the structuring of the object model at an early stage

• refining the services a system provides to a user.

CRC AND OMT

CRC (Class Responsibility Collaboration), as proposed by Kent Beck and explored more fully in Rebecca Wirfs-Brock's book of *Software System Development* (Wirfs-Brock *et al.*, 1990), is the second technique, and again is used very early on in the analysis of a system. It, too, can be used to understand the base structure of what are the important objects, what are the services and what is the response. Unlike use cases, however, which focus on the external aspects of the system, or black box, CRC focuses on the processes within, the white box view.

Early OMT modelling from the problem statement provides a list of nouns as classes, and verbs as relationships. CRC looks at the classes and services defined within the system and then focuses analysis on three questions:

- Class—What should objects be called, do we have a good candidate from the noun search?
- Responsibility—How is the work of the system divided between the objects?
- Collaborators—Which objects are required (collaborated with), for this object to provide its published service?

CRC developments are expressed in workgroups as a free form text description of each object. Each object is assigned an index card, and the cards are laid together on a table. Each card represents a class and has the services it provides written on it. The system workgroup then picks up the cards relating to the objects they are talking about, and these become the objects. By walking through the sequence of events caused by a particular scenario, the workgroup of users and developers then effectively simulate how each class responds as a part of a particular scenario as it is played out, with the people in the group pretending to be a selected set of classes and reasoning if they (that class) should respond to a particular request (message) from another class. This procedure can take place many times, with many scenarios, to correctly identify the classes and their relationships. Throughout the CRC process, the classes and services are entered onto the CRC cards. At the end of a session, when the classes and their services have been defined to everyone's satisfaction, the information can often be transferred straight from the CRC cards to a first cut Object Model, or used to refine an existing one.

CRC is thus a technique for finding and explaining objects. It is used early in analysis to foster group communication and quickly lay the foundations for future work. It is used to explain systems to new teams members, or for management reviews. It is also an excellent vehicle for teaching object oriented thinking, and refining the requirements of a system and critical use cases.

The OMT process produces a list of nouns and verbs to be used as classes and relationships within the OMT Object Model. These are then used in the analysis to produce either an object model, or in conjunction with scenarios an event trace diagram. When CRC is used as an enhancement to OMT, CRC steps in at the point at which there is a first cut object model. By the use of repeated questioning about the classes, their responsibilities and the collaborations required, CRC then enables the OMT object model to be refined.

The very early analysis phase of OMT could be visualised as shown in Figure 3. This conveys the general process of iterating between activities and diagrams. The numbered arrows infer an approximate sequence in which the various modelling activities would be carried out. But each development would have different emphases in its early stage and may iterate through the elements with different priorities.

The key model developed in OMT is still the Object Model, but supported by various interaction modelling elements. The Object Model is refined through the various phases of OMT from concept to code. The

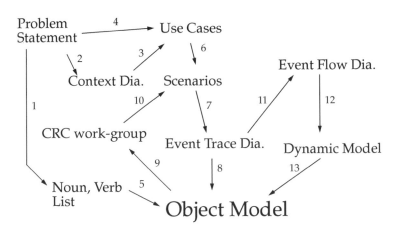

Figure 3   Flow Development of OMT

aim of this early work is to analyse, specify, and define the system which is to be built.

The initial phase now consists of:

- a Problem Statement

- a context diagram

- an object and relationships pick list

- use cases with text descriptions

- scenarios and event trace diagrams

- an Object Model

- an event flow diagram

- dynamic model for important and interesting classes.

The next model that is explored is the Dynamic Model. The refinement of scenarios and event trace diagrams are summarised in the Event Flow Diagram. This focuses attention towards the objects that are displaying the most dynamic behaviour. This is then captured using Harel state notation (Harel, 1987), indicating the constraints that may be required to be exercised by a given object when handling given sequences of events.

CAVEATS CONCERNING THE BLEND OF TECHNIQUES

Use case or scenario-driven analysis keeps ideas close to the usage of the system. However, this can as easily be a disadvantage as an advantage. The danger of scenario driven approaches is that the focus is too much around current needs, and this may compromise long-term flexibility. In addition, by concentrating too much on the way users currently work, it is possible for the analysis to miss the opportunities in re-engineering the business process. Business process redesign can bring far bigger benefits than mere computerisation, and may be carried out using an OMT style analysis. This provides a continuity of modelling to the enterprise. Data and event driven techniques, by focusing on essential processes rather than user-interactions, are better able to divorce the analyst from inefficient current practice. OMT can help to force that balance of modelling, gaining benefit from both approaches.

The concern about the use case/scenario approach is whether it is possible to effectively describe systems, particularly larger systems, without defining a data model. This is a point that is particularly relevant when considering that data models stress a data view which should be resilient to changes in its use. In this sense, the Wirfs-Brock and Jacobson techniques could be seen as similar to process-driven modelling, with the attendant danger that a change of requirements could lead to a fundamental change in the model. While Jacobson stresses the need to manage continual change via process, there is a diminishing return on invested knowledge if you need to restructure it all the time.

The assessment of which techniques in a method are useful and produce uniform results, and which meander off in a different direction each time they are used, is one of the most difficult areas to determine within a method. I am not an advocate of blending notations or models from different methods, but I do believe strongly that the techniques of one method may often be adopted in another method for greater benefit in refining the models.

CASE AND MODELS IN OO SYSTEM DEVELOPMENT

The availability of credible tool support for a given method is often the first key issue for an organisation, as it is virtually impossible to maintain a project of any size fully documented, consistent and up-to-date without effective tool support.

Many people suggest that tools are not required until a team of three or four are working together to maintain integrity of communications. Whilst this may be valid, projects of 1–3 may be equally at risk. If a person who leaves is the only member, or is one of the key contributors, often what is left behind in engineering logs or in machine directories is virtually impossible to find and decipher. They will often have been the only authority on that project information.

The concept of liveware can be very appealing to an individual in preserving his value to an organisation, representing the decryption key to a system or project. Modern software methods and tools make the secrecy aspect of liveware very difficult to maintain, thus removing the dependency on one person. The tools give visibility and communication to an organisation, and so are essential at all sizes of projects.

In larger projects there is a chance that others will know some, if not all, of their work, and their percentage contribution is often smaller. Therefore, from a management perspective, tools are essential, both to a large team for communication, and for the one man project for visibility and consistency of models. When large systems are developed, it is important that all documentation and models of the system be consistent. This means, among other things, that an object must be given the same name throughout the documentation, which can often be difficult to achieve. By means of a tool, a large number of the work tasks can be automated, especially trivial tasks that would otherwise become cumbersome due to their volume. If the work tasks in the underlying process are seamlessly interconnected, a great deal of the work can be automated, as the development progressively refines the result of a project.

Case tools are critical in this growing area of object oriented development. The ability to hold all of the diagrams in the various models and then navigate directly to a relevant area is important, as is the ability to check and maintain the consistency of the information entered. The question has been raised in the past, 'Would OO kill off CASE?' The total opposite is true. The success and interest in Object Technology, combined with a greater awareness of development process needed in OO development, is boosting the interest and requirement for CASE tools. Beyond the trivial level, a serious project cannot document, capture, communicate, check, manage and change the development of a modern OO project without massive time and personnel hours, if done manually. No-one today would believe that a carpenter could be cost effective if required to use only hand tools. So why do people believe that they could be effective with paper and pencils? It is rare today to see a mechanical drawing board in a modern drafting office, as they have all been replaced with modern computerised tools.

Browsing and reuse are also critical to projects and organisations in order to be cost effective in the future and to gain the true benefits of object re-use. IDE, in collaboration with the official mentors of OMT, the Advanced Concepts Centre of Martin Marietta, have created a powerful UNIX implementation of OMT – StP/OMT. Again, this is a sign of the maturing CASE market, that IDE is in direct collaboration for the evaluation and further definition of the OMT method. StP/OMT provides life cycle coverage from concept to OO code generation in various OO languages, for multiple user work groups and projects. Class capture of existing C++ code and libraries, with repository browsing facilities, makes access to and reuse of information very productive.

I believe that 'OO in 94' will be the view of the future. It will be the year that widespread corporate and project adoption of object technology takes off in Europe. It is interesting to note that traditional structured methods courses are rapidly being replaced by OO courses.

Empirically, OMT is becoming the dominant OO method. OMT

courses run publicly across the industry in the UK alone at two or three times a month. On-site project training is at the same level and growing. Every OO show brings new OMT CASE offerings to the market. OMT has over a dozen CASE tools providing various degrees of support. The contending OO methods at best can claim four or five tools in their camp, with no new releases apparent in the market. Organisations are also purchasing UNIX OMT CASE tools in volume, some with sets of 50 licences at a time. OO has come of age in 94, and CASE is essential to support OO system development for the methods to be effective.

CONCLUSION

This paper has discussed the value of adopting techniques of Use Case from Jacobson, and CRC from Wirfs Brock, and how they may refine the early development of OMT Object Model. Also proposed is why CASE is essential to the support of OO methods.

The consistent modelling notation within OMT allows detail to be captured and added to the evolving models. By applying techniques such as Use Cases and CRC responsibility, discovery and reasoning to the early development of the model evaluation, a more repeatable and consistent set of OMT models may be derived.

The very essence of the OO development process is: discovering and representing objects; finding and structuring good classification schemes that provide clear abstraction of the problem domain; allowing good behavioural normalisation; separating out the structures of objects to maximise reuse; and helping to reason about composition and inheritance of the system under development from its stated or inferred requirements. If a method does not provide or allow the use of techniques and models that allow the development of OO abstractions to become intuitive and a natural part of a consistent and repeatable development flow, it will become shelf-ware.

The early iteration of the problem statement in OMT is based on the aspect of identifying the objects and class of the system, based on the nouns of the system, to build the Object Model. While this can provide a valuable pick list of names for the classes, it can be difficult to refine which names are synonyms of others, and which may be the most relevant. I suggest that there is a natural synergy in OMT which already supports the concept of scenarios and event trace diagrams to Use Cases and CRC. This will provide a more mature and repeatable flow to early OMT development.

'Go with the flow but choose your techniques carefully.'

ACKNOWLEDGEMENTS

To Maria Kavanagh, my wife, for her methods insight and contribution to this paper, thank you.

REFERENCES

Harel, D. Statecharts: a visual formalism for complex systems, *Science of Computer Programming*, **8**, 231-274, 1987.

Jacobson I. *Object Oriented Software Engineering, A Use Case Driven Approach*. ACM Press, 1991.

Kavanagh D. Life-cycles, phases, and deliverables for an OMT project. *Proceedings TATOO*, UK, 1994.

Rumbaugh J. *et al*. *Object-Oriented Modelling and Design (OMT)*. Prentice Hall, 1991.

Rumbaugh J. Objects in the Twilight Zone, How to find and use application Objects. *J. Object Oriented Programming*, June 1993.

Wirfs-Brock R. J. *et al*. *Designing Object Oriented Software*. Prentice Hall, 1991.

6

*The Fusion*CASE *Experience*

Howard Ricketts

ABSTRACT

Fusion is rapidly establishing itself as a leading contender among a new breed of OO methods. Drawing on proven OO techniques, Fusion is a hybrid method which provides a clear and focused process leading from requirements analysis to code. Treating the system as a black box, Fusion considers the contracts the system must fulfil as a whole. This interface is then refined through consideration of scenarios—allowable threads of execution through the system. During design, responsibility for events arriving at the system is assigned to specific Classes which in turn delegate responsibility. Finally the visibility and inheritance aspects of Class relationships are modelled and classified to provide concrete Class Descriptions suitable for direct implementation.

In support of this method is *Fusion*CASE from SoftCASE Consulting. While continuing to grow in stature, *Fusion*CASE has gained widespread acceptance as the leading Fusion CASE tool both inside the Hewlett Packard community, the originators of Fusion, and outside. This paper provides an outline of the Fusion method and describes some of the architectural decisions taken in developing the *Fusion*CASE tool.

Business Objects: Software Solutions. Edited by Kathy Spurr, Paul Layzell, Leslie Jennison and Neil Richards
© 1994 John Wiley & Sons Ltd

NEW PLAYERS

The Fusion method first saw the light of day during 1992. Developed by Hewlett Packard Bristol Laboratories initially as an internal training aid, the Fusion method has matured into a concise and cohesive set of OO techniques underpinned by a systematic development process (Coleman *et al.*, 1993). Within Hewlett Packard Fusion has grown to become the hub of their OO training and support services. Despite this favourable pedigree, Fusion must however be viewed as a young and developing method. The first products developed using Fusion are now just starting to roll off the production line.

*Fusion*CASE can boast even less longevity. While available for evaluation during the later part of 1993, *Fusion*CASE first became commercially available during February 1994.

Jointly, therefore, Fusion and *Fusion*CASE must be seen as relatively young entrants in the fiercely competitive world of OO methods and CASE tools. This lack of history should not, however, detract from the quality of the underlying approaches and technology. *Fusion*CASE has been designed to deliver real leverage on OO projects, maximising the capabilities offered by Fusion, minimising manual tasks and automating most of that which can be automated.

FUSION AND *FUSION*CASE—MOTIVATIONS

Like its predecessors, the OO paradigm is still as much experimentation as science although it is clearly a better science. Better because of its focus on the entire software life-cycle not just the first cut of an application, and better because of its affinity to components which has proven successful in many other fields of problem solving.

Experimentation is a necessary step in the evolution of any science—it leads to improved understanding and will in time lead to a stable set of tried and trusted techniques. Fusion is the first attempt at integrating the more established and proven techniques found in the foremost OO methods into a single cohesive analysis and design method. With an eye on the practical, the originators of Fusion have stripped away much of the theoretical noise found in its forerunners to produce a clean, goal oriented method capable of sustaining rigorous use on large software development projects. Whether or not Fusion has the right constituent parts will be borne out over the coming years. However, Fusion has already been shown to work on large scale projects, and is increasingly being adopted as the preferred OO method with large and small organisations alike.

OO development has created its own breed of management problems. Many of the current OO methods (e.g. Coad and Yourdon, 1991a, b) expound the benefits of depth-first development with little regard for the implications for project management. The depth first model encourages parts of a problem to be analysed, designed and prototyped as a basis for establishing the scope of the system. The key benefits are therefore seen to come from prototyping—the demonstration through worked examples that the requirements have been understood. One problem this technique suffers from is that project managers cannot quickly establish the scale of the whole software engineering task—prototyping takes time and resources. One must effectively build a skeleton application before one can answer the questions 'How much is it going to cost or how long will it take?'. The early answer to these questions is normally a pre-condition to achieving business sign-off for a large scale development project.

Large scale development requires effective management which can only be achieved with well defined milestones, quantifiable progress and effective communication, i.e. through a rigorous and systematic process. The Fusion process (Figure 1) attempts to address these issues by reaffirming the distinction between the analysis, design and implementation phases and their associated deliverables. Having clear phases with predictable deliverables, which can be checked for completeness and correctness, ensures problems are detected earlier in the project life-cycle, allows effective problem partitioning (team working), and the preparation of qualified plans.

It is interesting to observe that the largest stone to be thrown at top-

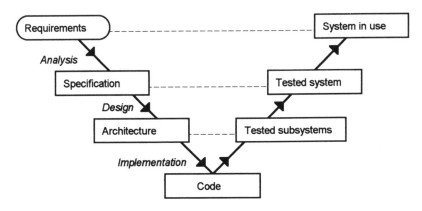

Figure 1   Phases of Software Development

down design can also be thrown at OO methods—'decisions are often made too early'. If the first act of developing a large application is to develop class abstractions, one runs the risk of identifying the wrong classes and therefore unmaintainable solutions. The issue is clearly not 'what elements make up the system' but 'what is the system supposed to do'. It therefore makes sense to defer the assignment of responsibility as late as possible. This again is a feature of Fusion.

To say that all other OO methods are overly complicated or inadequate would be a gross over-statement. The observation is simply that each has its strengths and weaknesses. It is these strengths which Fusion has attempted to draw together into a clear and cohesive method. Fusion is a hybrid method—it draws on OMT (Rumbaugh *et al.*, 1991) for the use of object models, formal methods for the description of the effect of external events on the system, Class Responsibility Collaboration (CRC) (Beck and Cunningham, 1989) for modelling object interactions and Booch for describing inter-class visibility. Underpinning these is a robust and systematic process.

FUSION—AN OVERVIEW

Analysis within Fusion is supported by three notations—Object Models, the Life-cycle Model and Operation Schemas. *Fusion*CASE has introduced a fourth—the System Context Diagram. Collectively, these notations are used to establish the system boundary and interface, i.e. those parts of the problem domain which lie inside the system and are to be implemented by software, and those which are not; the operations which the system as a whole must support; and the allowable sequences of system operations. In general, analysis may progress in any order, although typically one starts using Object Models.

An Object Model (Figure 2) is essentially an enhanced Entity Relationship Attribute diagram—enhanced in that it supports aggregation (things form *parts of* other things) and inheritance (one thing is a *kind of* another). Object Models are used to model the types of things which make up the problem domain (Classes) and their inter-dependencies (Relationships). In conjunction with the other analysis notations, one progressively refines the Object Models to define the nature of the system and system boundary.

The Life-cycle Model (Figure 3) is concerned with capturing how the system communicates with its environment, i.e. the events which flow from the environment to the system, and *vice versa*. Behaviour across this interface is modelled in terms of scenarios—allowable threads of communication between the system and its environment.

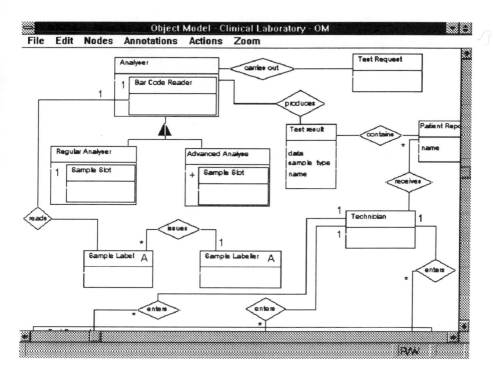

Figure 2   Object Model

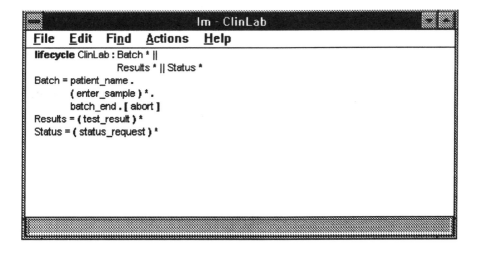

Figure 3   Life-cycle Model

The final element of analysis is the Operation Model (Figure 4). Each operation supported by the system has a corresponding Operation Model which declares how the execution of the operation changes the system state. Operation Models therefore start to look inside the system, i.e. at 'effect' rather than 'cause'. Using formal preconditions and post-conditions, each Operation Model gives a static declaration of system behaviour in terms of its effect on a number of notional objects which collectively define the system state.

The result of analysis is a set of classes which are candidates for design and a set of system operation definitions. Design is characterised by four notations—Object Interaction Graphs, Visibility Graphs, Inheritance Graphs and Class Descriptions.

Each Object Interaction Graph (Figure 5) builds on the information entered into a system's Operation Model. Taking the notional objects used to define system state a user can add additional notional objects or collections of objects in support of design. One object is set out as the

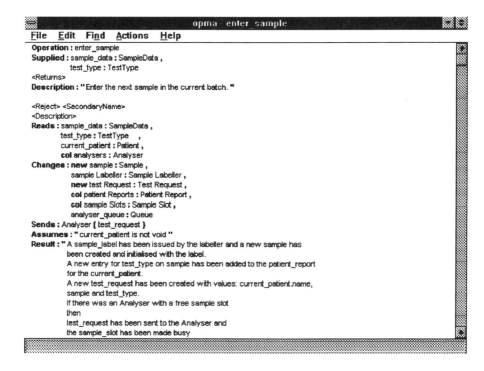

Figure 4 Operation Model

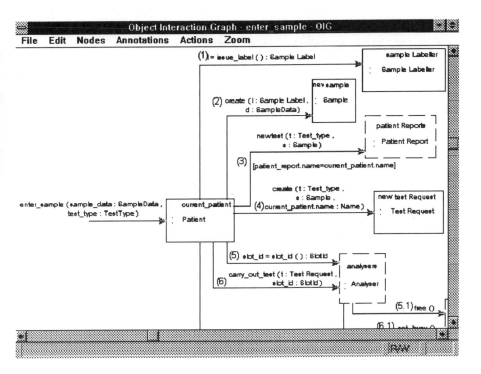

Figure 5   Object Interaction Graph

recipient of the incoming system operation and given responsibility for implementing the service. Implementation takes the form of calling upon the services of other objects in a specified order.

One object being able to call upon another for a service implies that the Class of client object has some form of visibility of the server object. Visibility Graphs (Figure 6) are used to capture and refine this notion of visibility. Fusion identifies four kinds of visibility: visibility arising from one Class owning objects of another (Server Binding), visibility which exists over a single method call (Reference Lifetime), visibility which is shared with other classes (Server Visibility), and visibility which can or cannot be changed after initialisation (Reference Mutability).

The results of design are captured in individual Class Descriptions (Figure 7). Although forming the basis for implementation in a programming language, Class Descriptions are not simply static documents. They are a repository for design decisions which may be further refined, e.g. in the identification of inheritance structures.

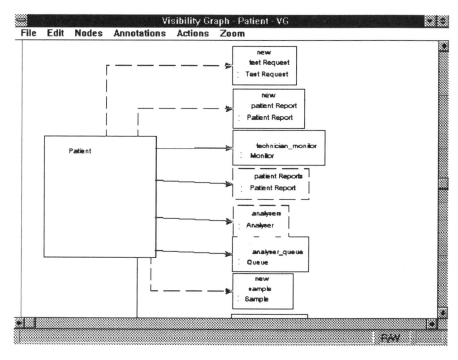

Figure 6   Visibility Graph

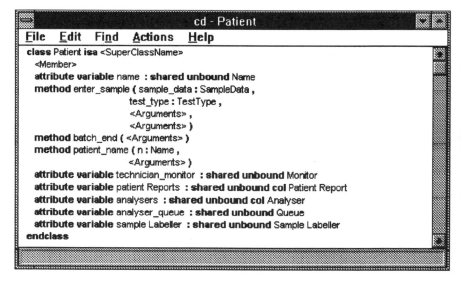

Figure 7   Class Description

Unlike many other OO methods which place great store on establishing inheritance structures at an early stage of design, Fusion delays this activity until well into design preferring to treat inheritance as an optimisation. This approach operates against the creation of a proliferation of highly nested inheritance trees by focusing the search for inheritance on commonalty of purpose rather than composition or functionality alone. Inheritance Graphs (Figure 8) are used to factor out commonalty (generalisation) and specialisation.

The final stage of Fusion is the transformation of design into an effective implementation. Here Fusion details the process rather than the language specific transformations although standard mappings for Eiffel and C++ are defined.

Fusion—Rounding off the Method

While clearly a significant step in the right direction, Fusion still has a few steps to go. The method includes some 'black holes'—concepts with

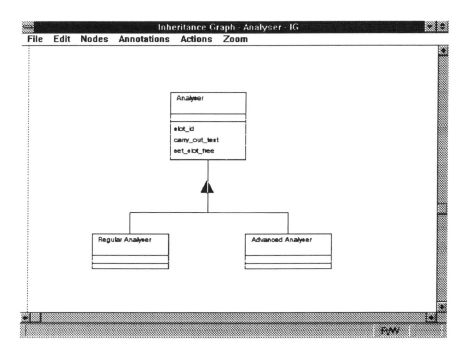

Figure 8   Inheritance Graph

no discernible forward traceability. Relationships and aggregates are good examples in that they exist in analysis but have no direct equivalents in design. In practice, a relationship can be implemented as a class, class attribute or more commonly as a class method. An aggregate should find its way to becoming a Bound Server visibility relationship. These minor holes are neither significant nor conspicuous and can in part be plugged through CASE support.

Over the coming years, Fusion is likely to develop in a number of strategic ways. To become widely used for the development of real time embedded systems Fusion will have to support the modelling of concurrency and some form of State Modelling. Practice has also shown that users find timeline diagrams particularly useful as a diagrammatic technique for modelling scenarios. One interesting aspect of Fusion is that these extensions could be included without disruption to the underlying process or existing notations suggesting that Fusion has separated the issues of timing, data and visibility well.

In conclusion, Fusion is a practical method designed to address large scale software development. It is likely to evolve with increased use and exposure to new problem domains. Some refinement is also needed to some of the existing concepts.

*FUSION*CASE—PAST, PRESENT AND FUTURE

SoftCASE Consulting is a small UK software house which specialises in the development of tailored CASE solutions. This business is based on our expertise in the application of meta-CASE technology for the production of CASE tools delivering strategic benefit. We believe this grounding in one-on-one consultancy provides us with unique insights into the problems facing CASE users and it is these insights which we have tried to bring to bear in the development of *Fusion*CASE.

*Fusion*CASE is SoftCASE Consulting's first venture into the tactical, off-the-shelf tools arena. Implemented on the GraphTalk meta-CASE technology, *Fusion*CASE is also marketed as an extendible CASE tool in that it can be configured to offer organisations strategic benefit through addition or adaptation of notations and integration with other tools, company practices or specialised architectures.

*Fusion*CASE is available in a number of flavours. The Small Project version allows organisations to evaluate Fusion and *Fusion*CASE simultaneously without having to commit large budgets. Users may then upgrade to the full Single User version or Team Working version. Two language toolsets (C++ and SmallTalk) are also soon to be released. Each toolset incorporates a language sensitive editor, code generator and a reverse engineering facility.

The Team Working version allows teams of developers to concurrently perform analysis and design in independent design sessions. Periodically these designs may be merged together to reconcile differences and to form the basis for a new baseline. This same strategy also supports version management through integration with external configuration management tools.

*Fusion*CASE is currently 'SoftBench encapsulated to level 3—ANSI X3H6 Standard'. At level 3 compliance, *Fusion*CASE guarantees an open tools interface—making it simpler for users to integrate with tools in the SoftBench Framework and plug-compatibility—ensuring users can switch from *Fusion*CASE to another standard analysis and design tool while maintaining functionality and operability with other tools in the environment. With increased standardisation in this area, *Fusion*CASE will continue to integrate with more and more lower CASE tools to form part of a heterogeneous development environment on SoftBench platforms. Other initiatives, such as CORBA, OLE etc. are also being closely tracked.

*FUSION*CASE—INSIGHTS INTO CASE TOOL DESIGN

CASE is now a well established industry which is populated by both good and bad tools. In developing *Fusion*CASE we have set out to place ourselves firmly in the former camp by attempting to deliver a tool which enhances the usefulness of the Fusion method through proactive support for the development process. Three strategies have been pursued:

- Detect and prevent errors at source.

- Automate all that may be usefully automated.

- Give assistance to the user wherever possible.

Normalised Data Dictionary

Central to *Fusion*CASE is the Data Dictionary. Implemented substantially as a normalised database, the Data Dictionary acts as the repository for all design data. Its Information Model consists of the Classes, Agents, System Operations, Inheritance and Visibility relations, etc. which make up Fusion. As a user builds up a design via diagrams and documents these concepts are extracted and stored in the Data Dictionary. In fact the Fusion notations, the diagram and document types which collectively define Fusion, can be thought of simply as views onto the Data Dictionary, i.e. sophisticated mechanisms for entering and viewing parts of the Data Dictionary (Figure 9).

A normalised Data Dictionary is a powerful concept as it centralises consistency checking between notations, minimises code and allows global changes to be made at a single point. From this approach stem the concepts of on-line consistency checking, context sensitive selection lists, enhanced navigation and automatic data propagation.

On-line Checking

On-line consistency checking actually comes in two flavours—syntactic and semantic (Figure 10). The term 'on-line' refers to the fact that the checks are applied interactively, i.e. as a user attempts to manipulate the design. This approach ensures that entered data is substantially correct and thereby reduces errors at source.

Syntactic checking concerns support for the notations, 'Can I connect one of these to one of those?', while semantic checking is concerned with data content, ' Given I have this can I do that to it?'.

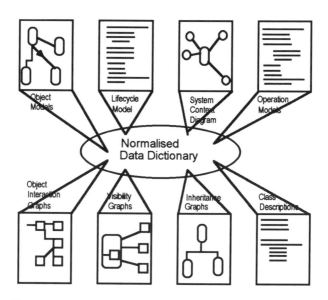

Figure 9 *Fusion*CASE Normalised Data Dictionary

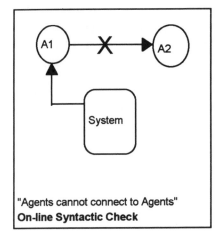

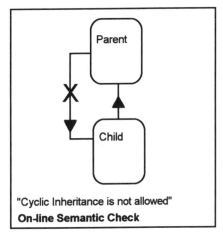

Figure 10   On-line Consistency Checking

Context Sensitive Selection Lists

An important productivity aid provided by *Fusion*CASE is context sensitive selection lists. When entering data, *Fusion*CASE allows a user to either enter a new value or choose an existing value from a dynamically generated selection list. The selection list contains only values which are valid in the current context.

The queries used to populate selection lists can become very complex. For example, when entering actual parameters for a method invocation on an Object Interaction Graph, *Fusion*CASE offers parameters which are first restricted by type and then by scope.

Data Propagation

Where a particular concept is shared across several diagrams or documents it is often possible to provide automatic data propagation. For example, each Agent which appears on an Object Model should be represented at least once on the System Context Diagram. Many to one relationships of this form therefore become excellent candidates for automatic data propagation. There are many examples of automatic data propagation in *Fusion*CASE—rename rippling is another good example.

There is often a natural tendency to view data propagation as being one directional—from analysis, through design into code (trace-ability is conventionally viewed in this direction). Unfortunately users have an unnerving habit of using CASE tools in ways that were not thought appropriate during their design. Accommodating this twist to Murphy's law, vendors should consider all candidate propagations. As a rule of thumb a CASE tool can provide automatic data propagation wherever one can say 'if it exists there it could also exist here'.

A good example of this theme in *Fusion*CASE concerns Class Descriptions (Figure 11). Fusion considers Class Descriptions to be entirely derived. Information regarding inheritance, visibility, composition etc. are extracted from other viewpoints and deposited in Class Descriptions as a prelude to code generation. While this mapping is clearly necessary, it is important to realise that it is not in fact one directional—creating or modifying a Class Description could just as easily instantiate inheritance, visibility and composition relationships. *Fusion*CASE utilises this fact in support of reverse engineering.

An important dimension to automatic propagation which is often overlooked, is consideration of 'negative logic'—destroying a concept can often have more serious implications than creating it. Many CASE tools simply treat destruction as the reverse of creation. This view of creation and destruction does not take account of the passage of time where

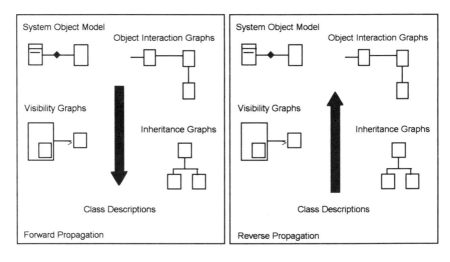

Figure 11   Forward and Backward Automatic Propagations

the existence or non-existence of some fact may seriously affect subsequent decisions. Consider a house being built, the laying of a brick at ground level is a pre-requisite for putting doors, windows, etc. on top. Removing a brick which has nothing on top is relatively inconsequential. However, having constructed the house, the removal of the brick is likely to lead to disastrous consequences. The same is true of creation and destruction of concepts in CASE tools.

The same problem arises with cut, paste and rename. *Fusion*CASE incorporates a generic language sensitive editor used to support the Fusion textual notations—the Life-cycle Model, Operation Models and Class Descriptions. Each of these documents is defined in terms of a regular tree-structured grammar. Using the editor one expands placeholders to reveal either more structure or terminal placeholders used for entering data values such as the names of Classes, Objects, Relationships, etc. Terminal placeholders therefore correspond directly to information stored in the Data Dictionary. Cutting a line of text within an editor cannot therefore be viewed simply as an editing function—the cut text may consist of Data Dictionary values whose existence and position within a document may be relevant to the entire design.

Enhanced Navigation

Treating Fusion diagrams and documents as views and storing single copies of data in the Data Dictionary also provides a mechanism for enhanced navigation. Having selected an entity within a diagram or document , you can automatically navigate to any other diagram or document for which the entity is the subject, e.g. select a System Operation on the Object Model and directly navigate to the corresponding Object Interaction Graph. This approach greatly enhances traceability, consistency and productivity.

Team Working with FusionCASE

The Team Working strategy adopted within *Fusion*CASE is based on a client-server or book-in/book-out model. Each user operates entirely within their own design space i.e. one does not share a design database among team members. From time to time a user may deposit or retrieve 'components' of a design into/from the 'outside world'. The outside world is supported by configurable Put and Get handles which are attached to a configuration management tool of the users choosing. The nature and make-up of components broadly follow the lines of Fusion diagram and document types.

Deviations from Fusion

While tracking Fusion very closely, *Fusion*CASE has been allowed to deviate from the method in a number of minor respects. A strong and pervasive element of the Fusion method is that of its underlying process. The documented Fusion process requires that analysis precedes design which in turn precedes implementation. This cascade model of development is highly suited to large scale software development but can be relaxed somewhat for smaller projects.

*Fusion*CASE therefore supports a process which combines the Fusion width-first process with the simpler depth-first approach. In practice users may do vertical design (depth-first) in conjunction with analysis (width first) but *Fusion*CASE supports the notion of analysis decisions taking precedence over those made in design. In practice, there are few conflicts between analysis and design but when they do occur, *Fusion*CASE allows the user to arbitrate, i.e. to enforce analysis decisions over design or allow analysis and design to diverge. QA checks can be used at any time to report on divergence between analysis and design.

*Fusion*CASE also has some areas of non-compliance with the Fusion method, the most significant of which is the lack of support for drawing a system boundary on an Object Model. At present, *Fusion*CASE does not support graphical nets, and it has therefore been necessary to invent an alternative notation to distinguish between Classes inside and outside of the system—Fusion fortunately also makes this distinction, calling Classes which use system services Agents and those providing them Classes. This and other minor deviations will be corrected in future releases of *Fusion*CASE.

CONCLUSIONS

In describing a CASE tool it is difficult to isolate the tool from the method. To a large extent the first aim of the CASE tool developer is to make the tool and the method synonymous. The second is to enhance the methods appeal through extensions in the tool. *Fusion*CASE is now moving into this second phase with extensions for bottom-up design, automatic code generation, reverse engineering and Team Working support.

At the same time Fusion marches on. Interest in Fusion continues to grow at a rapid pace. As with most OO methods, it is starting to be used in a number of diverse application areas including business modelling and banking. This, coupled with acknowledged real time limitations, is likely to result in some minor enhancements to Fusion in the near future. The recent formation of the Fusion Users Group involving both practitioners and vendors is also a necessary and effective step towards ensuring the viability of Fusion in the longer term.

*Fusion*CASE is certain to grow alongside Fusion—SoftCASE Consulting have made a long-term investment and commitment to its future. Generic improvements in the base technology and feedback from customers will be fed into the tool and should enforce *Fusion*CASE's claim to being the most compliant tool for the Fusion method.

ACKNOWLEDGEMENTS

*Fusion*CASE has been built using the GraphTalk/LEdit meta-CASE toolset from Parallax Software Technologies, Puteaux, France.

*Fusion*CASE would not have been possible without the guidance and assistance provided by Derek Coleman, Chris Dollin and Paul Jeremaes of Hewlett Packard Bristol Laboratories.

REFERENCES AND BIBLIOGRAPHY

Beck K and Cunningham W. A laboratory for teaching object oriented thinking, *Proceedings OOPSLA*, 1989.

Coad P and Yourdon E. *Object-Oriented Analysis, 2nd ed.* Yourdon Press, 1991a.

Coad P and Yourdon E. *Object-Oriented Design,* Yourdon Press, 1991b.

Coleman D, Arnold P, Bodoff S, Dollin C, Gilchrist H, Hayes F and Jeremaes P. *Object-Oriented Development —The Fusion Method,* Prentice Hall, 1993.

Rumbaugh J, Blaha M, Premerlani W, Eddy F and Lorensen W. *Object-Oriented Modelling and Design,* Prentice Hall, 1991.

Wirfs-Brock R, Wilkerson B and Wiener L. *Designing Object Oriented Software,* Prentice Hall, 1990.

7

Object-Oriented Techniques within Shell Research: Two Case Studies

Gemma R Overboom

ABSTRACT

Object orientation was introduced in 1985 at Shell Research Rijswijk for the development of human-computer interfaces. The object-oriented approach was found to be an excellent way of managing the complexity demanded by these systems. As a spin-off, a significant amount of source code has been re-used in subsequent projects. It was observed that a methodology to guide the development of these systems was very necessary. A number of object-oriented software development methods have therefore been evaluated on their practical usefulness in typical Shell applications. As a result, the Object-Modelling Technique (OMT) has been applied to the analysis and design of a computer system for simulating the flow of oil and water through rock samples. To identify the added value of applying such a methodology, the results of this exercise were compared with an existing object-oriented pore simulator,

Business Objects: Software Solutions. Edited by Kathy Spurr, Paul Layzell, Leslie Jennison and Neil Richards

which was developed without a systematic development method. OMT clearly aided an intuitive style of software development, particularly with respect to the software's understandability, maintainability and versatility. OMT has also been used in other projects within Shell Research Rijswijk and a project to identify the requirements of a computer system assessing the reliability and integrity of an offshore platform is discussed.

INTRODUCTION

Object-orientation (Budd, 1991; Meyer, 1988) is a software-engineering technique to construct computer programs in terms of objects appearing in the application domain. An object encapsulates data as well as operations for data interpretation. Objects may inherit data and behaviour from 'parent' objects, such as a racing car being a specialisation of a car. Many object-oriented tools and techniques have become available, such as programming languages, data models, methodologies, databases and software development tools.

Within Shell Research Rijswijk, human-computer interfaces have been developed according to the object-oriented paradigm during the past five years (e.g. Overboom, 1992a). The object-oriented approach was found to provide an excellent way of managing the complexity demanded by these systems. As a spin-off, a significant amount of source code has been re-used in subsequent projects (Overboom, 1992b). However, it was observed that a method to guide the development of these systems was very necessary. In this paper, we outline how we selected such a method and we discuss the application of object-oriented techniques in two applications: the simulation of flow through porous rock material and the assessment of reliability and integrity of production platforms.

WHICH OBJECT-ORIENTED SOFTWARE DEVELOPMENT METHOD?

Many object-oriented software development methods have been published recently because there has been a general recognition within the industry of the need to guide the development of computer systems that adhere to the object-oriented paradigm. The technical capabilities of some of these methods have been evaluated along with their practical utility in typical Shell applications.

A subset of the methods published in the open literature was obtained by eliminating all those with any of the following characteristics: those that are programming-language dependent, cover only a small part of the software development cycle, do not expect to have a substantial market share or are not easily accessible (e.g. in terms of documentation). This resulted in seven methods being selected for further study: Rumbaugh, Coad-Yourdon, Shlaer-Mellor, Wirfs-Brock, Booch, Martin-Odell and Wasserman. These methods were evaluated with respect to their support for (object-oriented) concepts, the techniques used to model these concepts, analysis and design strategy, and practical utility. Attention was paid to results from other surveys in the same area (Goor et al., 1992; Arnold et al., 1991; De Champeaux, 1992). For a brief summary of the findings, see the Appendix.

The Object-Modelling Technique (OMT) (Rumbaugh et al., 1991) was found to surpass its competitors and we have therefore recommended OMT for the analysis and design of Shell Research's (object-oriented) computer systems. OMT supports many concepts, a well elaborated set of techniques, a thorough strategy on the analysis and design process, and it is also good from a practical point of view.

OMT was developed at General Electric Research Centre. The method is based on a sound object-oriented analysis of a problem domain in terms of object, dynamic and functional models that are modified and extended during the design and implementation phases. In the analysis phase, the focus is on *what* the system should do. The design phases emphasise *how* the system can be constructed and implemented. An iterative approach is followed within and between the analysis, design and implementation phases.

APPLICATION 1: A FLOW SIMULATOR

We have applied OMT for the analysis and design of a computer system for the modelling of flow through porous media. The results of this exercise have been compared with an existing simulator, which was written in C++ (over 3Mb source code, about 45 classes) and was developed without a systematic development method. The computer system specified by employing OMT differs substantially from the existing pore simulator. This approach enabled us to identify the added value of applying such a methodology compared to an intuitive style of software development. This will be discussed below.

Object-Oriented Concepts

This section elaborates upon the object-model development for a pore simulator in order to demonstrate the use of the object-oriented approach. The OMT notation is used.

One can interpret the model shown in Figure 1 as follows: the pore simulator shows an experiment on a rock sample (a 'plug'), which is modelled as a three-dimensional network. As shown in the upper right corner of Figure 1, this network consists of a number of pore bodies (the

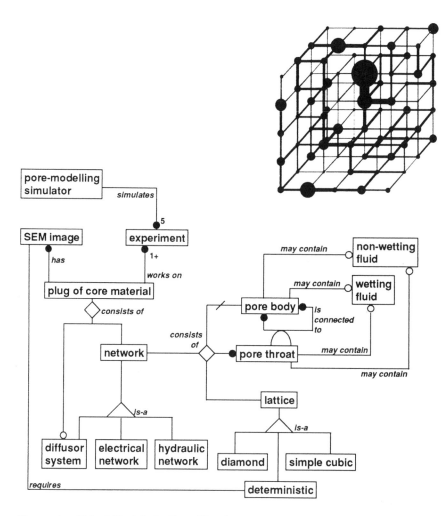

Figure 1 Object Model of a Pore Simulator

balls) connected by pore throats (the lines) arranged in a simple-cubic lattice. The lattice can also be diamond-shaped in structure. Alternatively, the lattice may be determined from a scanning electron microscope (SEM) image. Both the pore bodies and the pore throats may contain wetting or non-wetting fluids. Depending upon the experiments, the network may be considered as hydraulic (i.e. fluid flows through it) or as electrical (i.e. electricity can flow through the fluid in it). The object 'SEM image' contains only data, whereas the object 'experiment' contains both data and the operations needed to specify the experiment to be simulated. For the sake of simplicity, the data and the operations associated with each object are not shown here.

In Figure 2 each object is represented by a rectangular box, with the relevant data listed at the top of the box, and the operations or methods used to process these data at the bottom. The slash on the line joining the objects 'network' and 'pore body' means that the relationship between the two objects depends on other relationships, whereas the arc to the left of the 'pore throat' means that the pore throat governs the connection of one pore body to another.

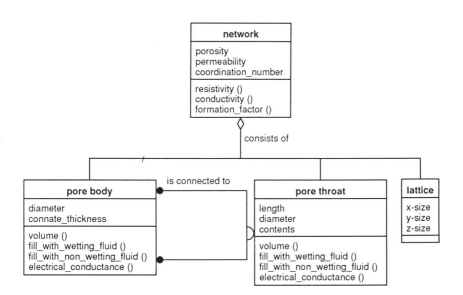

Figure 2   Detail of Figure 1, showing Data and Operations

Value of OMT

In this exercise, the value of OMT compared to using no methodology at all was clearly recognised, particularly with respect to the software's understandability, maintainability and versatility. We give the following reasons:

1. OMT expresses a problem using metaphors of objects appearing in the problem domain. This significantly simplifies communication with the domain expert. Nevertheless, the information analyst requires a basic understanding of the application domain. Intermediate documents can be discussed with the domain expert so that misunderstandings can be detected and repaired at an early stage in the software development process, thereby resulting in savings in cost and time.

2. Modelling is more than common sense. The guidelines and check lists provided by OMT are required to maintain the system's consistency. OMT also helps to shorten the object-oriented learning curve by a well-defined strategy, accompanied by many guidelines on how the techniques can best be used effectively.

3. OMT provides a framework for the management of software development. The progress can be measured, and the work can be farmed out among different software engineers.

4. Redundant information was incorporated in the implementation for efficiency reasons, such as state attributes, or the duplication of physical properties in a matrix structure to allow efficient processing. Often, the redundant information was found to be superfluous or could be hidden in the internal parts of the objects. In that way, optimisation does not hamper the re-use of objects in other applications.

Fortunately, large parts of the source code of the existing pore simulator could be re-used, to implement the OMT-derived system. In particular, the existing algorithms can be converted to fit within the new object hierarchy.

APPLICATION 2: RELIABILITY AND INTEGRITY ASSESSMENT OF PLATFORMS

Shell Research Rijswijk is investigating the integrity and reliability of subsea production systems, i.e. facilities gathering and transporting oil and gas from a well to an offshore platform. Subsea systems are composed of several components, such as flowlines, manifolds, Xmas trees and wells, each consisting of many more subcomponents. All these parts have specific properties, functions and failure conditions, besides which, many components also show similar failure behaviour (e.g. a family of valves). The probability of system failure can be determined by examining historical data and by comparing the actual operational loading with the, possibly degraded, load-resistance of system components. These so-called limit-state calculations are an important subject of research.

An Object-Oriented System Description

OMT has been used to specify the requirements of a computer system for the integrity and reliability of subsea production systems. The required information was obtained by interviewing the domain expert and studying available documentation about the problem domain. An object model (of about 90 classes) was made to describe the components of a subsea system, including their properties and behaviour.

A simplified object model where most properties and methods have been omitted is shown in Figure 3. A subsurface production system has been worked out with name and location as properties and with methods to create a system, to determine the components most prone to failure and to derive the probabilities of specific failures, such as leakage.

Subsequently, the processes leading to component and system failures have been expressed in the functional model. Here, the fault trees are combined with limit-state calculations. Part of the graphical representation of the functional model is shown in Figures 4 and 5, in which the probability of leakage of hydrocarbons through the casing is described. The ovals contain processes and the arrows show the input and output data they require. The grey ovals indicate that the process is described in detail in a subsequent diagram. For example, the process 'leak in casing' is specified in more detail in the second diagram of Figure 4. Figure 5 refines the limit-state calculations related to leakage through the casing.

Next to the functional modelling, the time-dependent behaviour of the system is depicted in the dynamic model. The analysis document serves as a discussion paper for future developments in reliability analysis of subsea systems. Some limit-state calculations have been

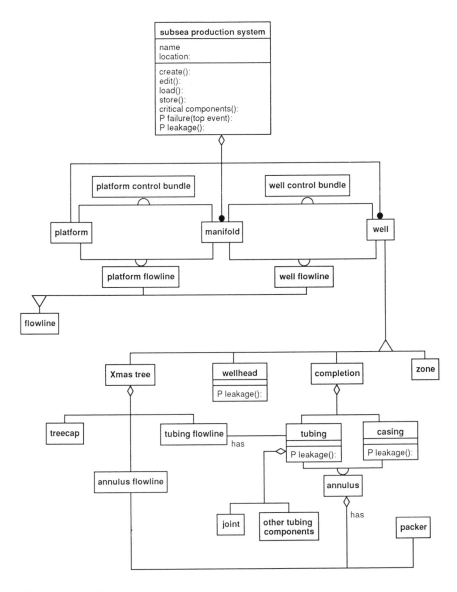

Figure 3   Outline of a Subsea System

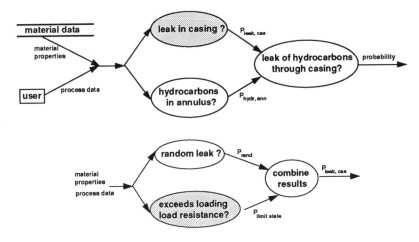

Figure 4   Functional Description of Leakage

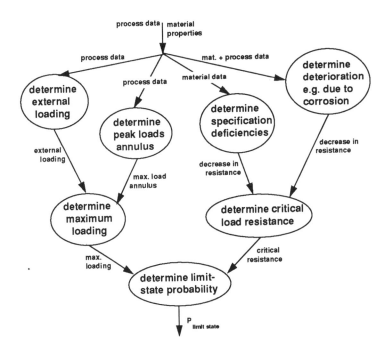

Figure 5   Zooming in further

worked out and others could also be included in the system in the same way.

Some observations

1. This approach facilitates the re-use of other developments in this area, such as limit-state algorithms and packages supplying the infrastructure or part thereof. In the design phase some opportunities to re-use software from other sources were explored.

2. The application of OMT significantly improved the communication between the domain expert and information technologist, since it allowed them to speak the same language. Although the domain expert has to invest some time in understanding the structure of the models, it pays off quickly. The domain expert can read, understand and comment on the object-oriented system specifications, enabling him to come to a precise, mutual understanding with the information technologist on system functionality prior to implementation.

CASE TOOL SUPPORT

Our investigations were geared towards selecting an appropriate methodology rather than a particular CASE tool, since we consider the philosophy underlying the methodology of higher importance than the way it is being supported by a tool. In addition, the object-oriented CASE tool market is rapidly changing. Now that object orientation provides an integrated analysis, design and implementation process, CASE tools which also support the implementation phase are within reach. Currently, many tools are sophisticated versions of a drawing package and do not appreciate the underlying methodology to the full extent. For example, they do not assist the user in the analysis and design strategy.

In application 1 Coad-Yourdon's OOATool was evaluated and it was found to be incapable of handling a realistic application. In particular, the automated positioning of objects on a worksheet was far from usable due to a poor routing algorithm. Moreover, the interactive performance was unacceptable. At that time there was no CASE tool available to support OMT and therefore, we chose not to use any CASE tools.

In application 2 we used the computer package OMTool (OMTool, 1993) that assists in the development of the information model via OMT. The tool was used throughout this project and provided useful support for the development of the object model. Via an intuitive graphical user-interface, a novice user quickly becomes acquainted with the tool. The C++ code generation facility that produced bug-free code was very useful, particularly for inexperienced C++ developers. Moreover, manual additions to the generated C++ code are preserved in subsequent code generation steps. OMTool generates a graphical representation of the object model as well as a report with a text description. Unfortunately, the report-generation facility is poor with a rigid format and document layout. In addition, the tool does not yet cover all aspects of OMT's object modelling, nor the development of dynamic and functional models. Other missing items are version management, support for reverse engineering and a mechanism to exchange OMTool models with other CASE tools. Altogether, OMTool is a useful product and good value for money.

CONCLUSIONS

We have come to the following conclusions:

- Object-oriented techniques have proven to be very useful for the development of applications within Shell Research.

- Based on a survey of seven object-oriented analysis and design methods, the Object Modelling Technique was selected as most appropriate. In this survey the focus was on practicality rather than mathematical foundation.

- OMT has been applied in two case studies, demonstrating its usefulness particularly with respect to its ease of employment within our environment, its completeness and its readability for non-information-technology specialists.

- We have experienced that modelling is more than common sense and a methodology certainly has added value compared to applying none at all.

- We have employed OMTool, one of the first CASE tools supporting OMT, and found it good value for money. Even in small projects, the benefits of using such a tool are already apparent. However, there is ample scope for improvement, particularly with respect to full support for OMT, adaptive report-generation facilities, version management, reverse engineering and C++ generation capabilities.

APPENDIX   AN EVALUATION OF SEVEN OBJECT-ORIENTED METHODS

The appendix briefly summarises the results of the evaluation of seven object-oriented software development methods, *viz.* Rumbaugh, Coad-Yourdon, Shlaer-Mellor, Wirfs-Brock, Booch, Martin-Odell and Wasserman. These methods have been evaluated with respect to four criteria: their support for (object-oriented) concepts, the techniques used to model these concepts, analysis and design strategy, and practical utility.

While most object-oriented software-development methods are still in the process of evolving, some convergence can be observed. All follow an iterative approach to software development as opposed to the traditional waterfall approach. In this way, prototyping is implicitly supported. All methods involve some form of object, dynamic and functional modelling; for most methods, a case tool is available to support this modelling. All methods suffer from a lack of precision because of their informal nature. This can be alleviated by the imposition of precise semantics on the method, such as a formal specification language.

Table A1 summarises how the methods perform against the four criteria formulated above. This table is ranked according to the results. The relative measure of a method for a feature indicated by '✔' is used to compare the methods with each other (i.e. to compare table elements of a single column). It cannot be used to compare the support of a method for features A and B (i.e. compare table elements of a single row!). For example, Coad-Yourdon supports a reasonable number of (object-oriented) concepts, provides only a small set of techniques to express these concepts, has a good strategy on how to proceed with the analysis and design, and has good practical value. However, one *cannot* conclude that Coad-Yourdon puts more emphasis on strategy than on concepts.

Figure 6 Summary of Findings

	Concepts	Techniques	Strategy	Practicality
Rumbaugh	✔✔✔	✔✔✔	✔✔✔✔	✔✔✔✔
Booch	✔✔✔✔	✔✔	✔✔✔	✔✔✔
Shlaer-Mellor	✔	✔✔✔	✔✔✔	✔✔
Coad-Yourdon	✔✔	✔	✔✔✔	✔✔✔
Martin-Odell	✔✔✔	✔✔✔	✔	✔
Wasserman	✔✔✔	✔✔	✔	✔✔
Wirfs-Brock	✔	✔	✔✔	✔✔

Concepts

The methods all support a comparable set of concepts in ways that are in accordance with the object-oriented paradigm. Booch supports the most elaborate set of concepts, closely followed by Rumbaugh, Martin-Odell and Wasserman (see Figure 6).

Techniques

The techniques underlying the methods are sometimes very different, especially in the design phase where the methods supporting design do not have much in common. Often, techniques used by the methods have been adopted from traditional software development methods (Jackson, 1983; Yourdon, 1989; Eilers, 1990) and modified to be fit-for-purpose in an object oriented environment. Particularly, most methods use a modified entity-relationship modelling (Chen, 1976) to model the static aspects, state-transition diagrams for the time-dependent behaviour within and between objects, and data-flow diagrams to describe functional dependencies.

Most methods originating from the structured analysis and structured design (SA/SD) community have a strong entity-relationship modelling part and most of them also provide data-flow diagrams. However, compared to SA/SD methods there is greater emphasis on data modelling and, therefore, the object-oriented methods are more suited for designing database applications. Methods inspired by ada pay more attention to real-time issues (e.g. deadlocks, constraints and properties), object communication and behaviour analysis.

Rumbaugh, Martin-Odell and Shlaer-Mellor compete for the best availability of techniques for assisting the modelling process (see Figure 6).

Strategy

The strategy that is followed in the analysis and design of a system is particularly important for the information analyst who does not have much experience in object-oriented modelling. It guides the analyst through the steps of this plan of attack and, more or less, ensures that a proper information system is developed in the end. Rumbaugh pays most attention to the strategy, followed by Coad-Yourdon, Shlaer-Mellor and Booch (see Figure 6).

All methods use an iterative approach in software development instead of the traditional waterfall approach. In contrast to traditional methods, they mix a top-down approach with bottom-up development.

Sometimes parts of the strategy are adopted from traditional methods and then modified. Martin-Odell combines a description of the strategy with an explanation of the concepts. This is very confusing and hampers the use of this method, particularly for an inexperienced user. However, a clear strategy is provided for the handling of events.

Practicality

It is, in general, difficult to evaluate the last criterion of practicality. It depends very much on the environment as to which method is most practical. We have given priority to:

1.   The available resources (books, CASE tools, courses) and their quality.

2.   The method's understandability.

3.   The value of the output for non-IT—as well as IT—professionals.

4.   The extendability of the models.

5.   The way in which the models are mapped on a programming language or database.

The degree of formality did not contribute to the ranking. Our view on practicality has resulted in the scores given in Figure 6.

From a practical point of view, Rumbaugh, Coad-Yourdon and Booch seem to be the most appropriate methods (see Figure 6). However, which method will be most appropriate depends heavily on the context of use. It is most effective if a software development team already has substantial knowledge of and experience with a method to utilise that method, unless they are not satisfied with it. For the development of technical applications within an environment of Fortran and C programs, Rumbaugh and Booch are more appropriate than their competitors.

Recommendation

The Rumbaugh method has the best overall score with respect to the four criteria we employed (see Figure 6). It is an excellent method that supports many concepts (only surpassed by Booch), provides an elaborate set of techniques to describe the information system and has a thorough strategy on the subsequent steps to be taken in the analysis and design process. In addition, it is a good candidate from a practical point of view. The many guidelines make the method useful for software scientists that still have to become acquainted with object orientation. We would like to point out that it is impossible to recommend a method that will give the best results under all circumstances. For example, for real-time environments the method of Shlear and Mellor is probably more suitable. Besides, many of the evaluated methods are still under development.

In our environment it is important that the method can handle rapidly changing requirements, incremental software development, prototyping, traditional implementations (i.e. mapping onto SQL and Fortran), and that it leads to operational products. Moreover, it should be usable to computing staff from a varying background. Within this context, OMT was most appropriate.

ACKNOWLEDGEMENTS

We much appreciate the input from E P Romsom and L C van Helvoirt on petrophysics and engineering, respectively. We thank P R Maarleveld for his valuable technical input.

REFERENCES

Arnold P, Bodoff S, Coleman D, Gilchrist H and Hayes F. *An evaluation of five object-oriented development methods.* Hewlett-Packard Laboratories, 1991.

Budd T. *An Introduction to Object-oriented Programming,* Addison Wesley, 1991.

Chen P. The Entity-Relationship model—Toward a unified view of data. *ACM TODS,* 1 1976, pp 9-36.

De Champeaux D and Faure P. *A comparative study of object-oriented analysis methods.* Hewlett-Packard Laboratories, 1992, pp 21-33.

Eilers H B. *Systeemontwikkeling volgens SDM,* Academic Service, 1990.

van den Goor G, Hong S and Brinkkemper S. *A comparison of six object-oriented analysis and design methods.* Method Engineering Institute, University of Twente, 1992.

Jackson M A. *System Development,* Prentice Hall, 1993.

Meyer B. *Object-oriented Software Construction,* Prentice Hall, 1988.

OMTool User Manual, General Electric Advanced Concepts Center, 1993.

Overboom G R. A novel approach towards user-interface technology in well-performance simulation. *Revue de l'Institut Français du Pétrole,* 47(3) 1992.

Overboom G R. The application of object-oriented techniques within Shell Research. *Conference Proceedings NOVI,* 1992.

Rumbaugh J, Blaha M, Premerlani W, Eddy F and Lorensen W. *Object-oriented Modelling and Design,* Prentice Hall, 1991.

Yourdon E N. *Modern Structured Analysis,* Yourdon Press/Prentice Hall, 1989.

8

Tool Support for Object-Oriented Development Methods

Philip Carnelley

ABSTRACT

Object-oriented technologies hold great promise for improving the development and delivery of information systems. However, achieving this promise requires the use of an object oriented approach in all phases of systems development. Indeed, the development process itself needs to be revisited, in order to produce a reuse-oriented approach leading to organic growth of systems. The top-down, information engineering style of approach that predominates in the industry today leads to large-scale rewrites rather than assembly of reusable components. Although these management and process issues are still the subject of debate, it is not too early to begin using currently available object oriented development methods.

This is best achieved using software tool support. Yet many current tools, and the methods they support, are wedded to the thinking of the

Business Objects: Software Solutions. Edited by Kathy Spurr, Paul Layzell, Leslie Jennison and Neil Richards
© 1994 John Wiley & Sons Ltd

1980s, and despite often being implemented using object oriented technologies, do not fully exploit object technology. There is also debate on the relative merits of basing developments on application development environments or focusing on analysis-oriented CASE products. This paper argues for a merging of the two approaches, to produce the best of both worlds. The directions of the CASE tool vendors, large and small, are fairly clear, and this paper will examine the merits of the vendors' strategies, present and emerging offerings, in the context of the overall development process requirements.

THE CHALLENGE: BUILDING SYSTEMS FROM OBJECTS

Since stored programs for computers were first devised, the search has been on for improved ways of creating those programs. That this search needs to continue is not in doubt. object oriented technology is generally recognised to be a major step in the right direction, for several reasons. In particular, its use is expected to lead to the situation where systems can be created almost instantly from existing components and subsystems, inter-operating through well-defined, compatible interfaces. The analogy with the 'Lego' children's building blocks is often made to illustrate this. Yet such 'plug-and-play' requires several advances in methods and tools that are not yet made. object oriented programming languages are not in themselves sufficient: while increasing productivity, they have to be used in the right context, they require expert programmers, and thorny issues remain, including large systems design, systems maintenance, quality assurance, and project management. We need suitable methods to support object oriented development, coupled with high-level tools.

There are of course several approaches to improving systems development, including fourth-generation languages, specification automation and other application generation techniques. However object-orientation is unique in its ultimate goal of producing new systems through assembly of components, off-the-shelf where possible, components which are reused a number of times without major rework. This approach can yield a step change in productivity (giving lower cost of production, and much shorter production times); it can heighten user satisfaction, especially where the user is free to assemble systems to his or her own requirements; and it can improve quality through the use of pre-tested components.

Consequently, larger-scale systems, where the need is greatest, need not be written and re-written from scratch in gargantuan, one-off projects taking years—and ultimately failing because in the interim, the need has changed. Rather, they will grow *organically*, like a city grows from a small town and its surrounding villages (Bowles, 1993). But there's the rub: to grow a city that works requires some element of town planning, procedures, rules and standards, infrastructure and firm foundations. Workers growing the city need a framework in which to work, and tools to work with, in designing and shaping the final outcome.

Importantly, then, any suitable approach needs to be able to make use of, or work with, existing applications and databases. Complete rewrites of core systems is a luxury few can afford, and in most cases, key applications will be implemented using packages. Conventional approaches have not addressed this re-engineering problem very successfully, and it appears that the object oriented model will be more effective, if this is a goal of the emerging methods. So far, however, object oriented methods and tools have not progressed very far in this direction.

THE REUSE REQUIREMENT FOR METHODS, TOOLS AND PROCESSES

It is fairly clear, then, that the objects route calls for creation of systems in an evolutionary manner, through the creation and then the large-scale reuse of components—objects and combinations of objects—which are created in such a manner that they make possible, even easy, such reuse. This in turn calls for methods and appropriate tools, to identify, design, build and document those objects and combinations of objects, giving components which are reuse-oriented. It further calls for methods to design and build complete systems with reuse as the major driver: this will include reuse of existing sub-systems in addition to reuse of components specifically designed for such a purpose.

The major requirement on the method should be to incorporate reuse at all stages of systems development. The method should also make possible studying a system from different viewpoints, at different levels of abstraction. Some reuse will be at a high level, complete subsystems reused without internal modification. Some will be at a detail level, using small but well-designed objects to implement specific functions. The requirement on tools is, at a superficial level, very simple: to assist with and automate the use of the method.

Popular object oriented analysis and design methods of today address some of these issues, but generally leave the question of reuse to the design stage, the build stage, or worse, leave it to the discretion of the implementors. They may assume it will just happen because they advocate a spiral process model of development (Booch, 1993, after Boehm, 1988). The recognition that a spiral model for the process, or, better, a fountain model (Henderson-Sellers, 1992) is a more natural reflection of how designers work, and should work to achieve reuse effectively, was a notable step forward. This idea, of iterating round the analyse-design-implement route, has been generally acclaimed. Yet most methods available today make only a passing reference to the revised process, rather than making it a centrepiece of the approach. They are not reuse-*driven*.

To see the folly of this, take an architectural analogy. An architect may be working on a greenfield site, but when drawing up plans, is this without thought to how it will be built? Of course not. Our architect will have in mind from the outset what components are available to build it, designing around standard-size bricks, doors and windows, unless there is a very good reason not to. What would be thought of a house that called for non-standard plumbing and pipework just because the standard dimensions had not been used at an early stage? The cost, and the building time, would be out of all proportion to any benefit gained. Also, the 'greenfield' site is a rare luxury. Most work is in the context of existing buildings and structures.

It is interesting to note, having drawn this analogy, that much of an architect's training is spent on studying previous best practice through the ages, which is not the case for software engineers. (An architect's training period is rather longer than for most other degrees). A greater emphasis on the reuse of design strategies during training would surely lead to an increasing practice of reuse when designing and building systems. This is illustrative of the significant change of perspective needed to properly embrace the reuse-driven, object oriented approach.

CURRENT METHODS—LOOKING FORWARD OR LOOKING BACK?

Most of the popular object oriented methods used and documented today are in fact a collection of techniques rather than complete methods, and are clearly rooted in the perception that their main task is to help analyse a new system's requirement and then devise a solution—implicitly, at least, this is a solution from scratch.

The major advance of the object approach is to take a holistic view of the components of a system, modelling them in their three dimensions of function, behaviour and data. In this way, object oriented methods take the best of 1980s thinking and improve it. Yet they are immature. They do not match fully the needs of building large, transactional business systems. In them, database design is not rigorous or fully-worked out, particularly in the case of non-relational database systems. A particularly difficult problem, which is not fully understood and is causing potential users much concern, is the separation of function and data, which is a part of using current database management systems (DBMSs). Indeed, DBMSs grew out of the conviction that such separation was beneficial— an idea somewhat at odds with the object oriented approach. Also, present object methods say little on transactional analysis or user inter- face and dialogue design—with the notable exception of the use-case approach in ObjectOry (Jacobson, 1992). This, perhaps the most innova- tive element of the whole batch of object oriented methods, takes a novel approach to the complexity problem by analysing the system from many different observers' (i.e. users') viewpoints. Some designers and method- ologists have tried to blend this particular technique with other methods.

Evolutionary and Revolutionary

Ovum's early research, (e.g. Jeffcoate, 1992) showed that up until recently few object oriented projects used any recognised object oriented analysis and design method, and companies were most likely to use an in-house or informal approach. Of the known and documented methods, however, three were generally recognised to be the most popular: Booch (1993), Shlaer-Mellor (1988) and Coad-Yourdon (1991). Subsequent work (as yet unpublished) leads us to believe that Booch and Object Modelling Technique (OMT—Rumbaugh, 1991), are increasing in popularity, but Coad-Yourdon and Shlaer-Mellor's positions are waning. Subsequently, newcomers have been few, but two methods are receiving attention: Hewlett-Packard's Fusion (Coleman, 1993) and ObjectOry. Another that is likely to receive attention and support over the next few years is object oriented Information Engineering, or OOIE (Martin, 1992), which is an umbrella term to describe efforts to blend the more traditional, top-down, data-driven approach known as Information Engineering (Martin, 1990) with the holistic, interoperability benefits of the object paradigm. Some commentators hold that these two approaches are mutually incompatible, but the debate is not yet resolved! Two methodologists in particular are working on this (separately), James Odell at Intellicorp in the U.S. (co- author of Martin, 1992) and Keith Short at Texas Instruments Information Engineering in England (Sanders, 1992). They have the advantage that what they produce will be implemented in CASE tools which are likely to be adopted widely.

All the methods mentioned so far may be described as *evolutionary*. That is, they have built on, and adapted, the approaches and thinking of the last 20 years and modified and blended the techniques and notation to produce something which seems to support the new technologies. Early results of using such methods has not produced notably better results than more traditional methods, as is borne out in Ovum's studies (Jeffcoate, 1992). It is also fair to say that the current approaches are fairly similar and that the similarities outweigh the differences. However there are distinguishing features such as notation, coverage and detail, which account for their relative popularities.

There is another camp, sometimes called *revolutionary*, which attempts to build from the inside out, as it were; to take the object (or object class) as the starting point, and describe systems from the object viewpoint. This is sometimes called *component engineering*. A major technique of this camp is that of class-responsibility-collaboration (CRC) first devised by Beck and Cunningham (1989), to analyse an object class's role in a system. This is an anthropomorphic view of the objects, which leads to interesting ways of analysis and design (such as role-play) and gives the most truly holistic view of the objects. An important criticism of the evolutionary methods is that the integration of the three dimensions into one object description is done at an arbitrary point and even in an arbitrary manner. The revolutionary methods attempt to avoid this.

There are three such methods that have drawn attention, though none has achieved widespread use, at least in part because of a lack of tool support. Each comes from a company closely identified with the Smalltalk language, and they are Object Behavior Analysis, first devised by Elizabeth Gibson (1990), and now being developed at Parcplace Systems (Goldberg and Rubin, 1993); Responsibility-Driven Design (Wirfs-Brock, 1990), now promoted by Digitalk; and Co-Design (Adams, 1992a, b) developed at Knowledge Systems Corp. Co-Design takes component engineering to another level, by widening the definition of the object to take in its documentation, its test specification and so on, and Knowledge Systems has also devised tools to manage such objects. Despite the lack of take-up, these 'revolutionary' methods appear better suited to supporting the 'plug and play' approach to systems construction but are weaker in dealing with the complexity of large systems.

Method Trends

In general, forward movement of current methods towards the construction mindset is apparent, although not as fast as this observer would like! There will be a shift away from top-down orientation (identifiable with the evolutionary approach) to accommodate bottom-up techniques (identified so far as revolutionary). Experience leads this author to believe that most successful projects blend top-down with bottom-up, and object-orientation does not change this. There will be a movement to see the development in terms of tasks, which may be concurrent, rather than phases which have a time sequence connotation. Increasing emphasis will be placed on buying rather than building (maybe from a market internal to the company) as libraries become available, and methods must give guidelines on the appropriateness of such a course, and how best to integrate those components. Ironically, methodologists make no assumptions about the capabilities of supporting tools and current methods could be implemented with only pencil and paper, albeit somewhat tediously. This will surely change in time.

As mentioned earlier, viewing existing systems in terms of objects shows promise as an approach to incorporating them into new requirements. Present re-engineering techniques have only been moderately successful in reusing data design information for use in new systems. More work on this topic is necessary (and likely).

CURRENT TOOLS—THE GREAT DIVIDE

Having examined how methods are developing to meet the object challenge, we can turn our attention to the question of how tools support development of object oriented systems. Software tools for object oriented development can be classified into three categories: programming support systems, application development environments and CASE tools. (For the purposes of this paper, 'CASE tools' is taken to mean tools which support—at least—a recognised analysis and design method.) These give an increasingly higher level of abstraction at which to work, potentially, in the order listed. They can therefore give a correspondingly higher benefit in terms of productivity and quality.

Programming Support Systems

There are several good toolsets to support use of the major object oriented programming languages: they include HP's Softbench and Centerline's CodeCenter, for C++; the Smalltalk programming systems from Parcplace and Digitalk; and ISE's Eiffelbench for Eiffel is also very good though not very popular, for marketing rather than technical reasons. They generally offer a tightly-linked, co-operating suite of tools to edit, compile, build and debug applications in a particular language. However, while using these can lead to the significant benefits that come from using an object oriented language, we can do better.

Application Development Environments

Application Development Environments (ADEs) can be thought of as fourth-generation environments for objects. They support programming at a higher level of abstraction (e.g. using a mouse to 'point-and-click' on icons representing advanced functions), with facilities to interactively define an application's graphical user interface, its data structures, and so on. Some, due to their roots in the artificial intelligence community, offer other options such as case-based reasoning and inferencing over object structures. These include Intellicorp's ProKappa and Inference's ART*Enterprise. Some tools support a conceptual split between object 'producers' and object 'consumers', i.e. between those who design and implement object classes, and those who want to satisfy a business problem as far as possible using what's available now. Notable examples are Digitalk's PARTS and IBM's rather similar VisualAge.

ADEs are undoubtedly powerful and have much to offer, but do not in general have much to offer on analysis and design. They tend to discourage a formal, managed approach with up-front requirements analysis, in favour of an informal, iterative approach making heavy use of prototyping and user demonstration/feedback to converge on an acceptable solution. ADEs can encourage reuse, because implementors will tend to use existing objects to speed up building of the prototypes if—and this is a big 'if'—they are aware that suitable objects are available. ADEs can provide mechanisms for locating and integrating objects into an application. This is especially true of PARTS and VisualAge. New objects are constructed to suit the needs of the moment. While generally effective, this is not necessarily the most cost-effective solution, and relying solely on ADEs lacks support for a coherent overall development plan. Sharing of objects, and general support for team working, are not a strength.

Unfortunately, ADEs are often chosen as an alternative to using a tool which supports object oriented analysis and design—our third category. Figure 1 lists representative tools from each class, and the strengths and weaknesses of the ADE approach compared to the classical CASE tool approach. As can be seen, in many ways they are complementary.

CASE Tools for Objects

The use of the word CASE (Computer-Aided Software Engineering) to

	CASE	ADE
+	Industrial strength Supports known methods Reengineering can utilise design legacy I-CASE can generate apps from integrated design repository	Flexible - often interpretive Incremental compile and execute Use bottom up or top down
−	Tied to methods or approaches of the past Weak support for revolutionary methods/future ideas	Immature for large teams Non-standard languages Legacy integration Unstructured approaches encouraged/ non-rigorous
E.g.	ObjectTeam Software Through Pictures Excelerator ROSE IEF (Future Versions)	PARTS VisualWorks ART*Enterprise Enfin ProKappa

Figure 1 Relative Merits of CASE Tools and ADEs

describe a class of tool has fallen into some disrepute of late, and even its meaning is in doubt. There are many such tools on the market supporting the major methods which were mentioned above. A fairly comprehensive list of available tools is given in Figure 2, but this is not the last word on this subject, as new entrants appear frequently.

The basic rationale for using such tools is to support the analysis and design task, having chosen from one of the available methods (and *not* the other way around!) So we must ask ourselves, how well do the current tools satisfy that requirement, is this a sufficient requirement for a good tool, and could they be better?

Failures of Vision...
The answer is that some are better than others, but they could all be better! The current crop of tools falls short on two levels. First, they are limited by the shortcomings of the methods they support, as listed above. Tool vendors are reacting to the methodologists and not taking advantage of features they may be able to offer because of the fact these are inherently computer-based tools, such as automatic scanning for reusable

Product	Vendor	Supports								Other OO	Platforms
		Booch	Coad/Yourdon	HOOD	OOIE	OMT	OOSD	Shlaer/Mellor	RDD		
Atriom	Semaphore	*								Semaphore, OSA	P,W,U
EasyCASE Plus	Evergreen										P
Excelerator 2	Intersolv					*		*		ObjectOry	D,U
HOOD Toolset	CASET			*				*			M,U
Iconix PowerTools	Iconix							*			D,U
IPSYS Toolbuilder	IPSYS Software	*		*				*			M
Macanalyst Expert	Excel Software	*									U, W, M
OBATool	Georg Heeg									OBA	U
Object Editor/LOV	Verilog										W,O,U
Object System/Designer	Palladio	*						*			U,W
Object Team	Cadre		*			*					P
Object-Designer	Chen & Associates									Chen	U
Objecteering	Softeam									Class relation	W
ObjectIF	MicroTool										U
ObjecTime	ObjecTime		*							ROOM	U,W
ObjectMaker	Mark V Systems	*		*		*		*	*	Various	M
ObjectModeler	Iconix	*	*					*		Objectory	W,O,M,U
ObjecTool	Object International		*								M,P,U
Objectory	Objective Systems									Objectory	U,W
OM Tool	Advanced Concepts Center					*					U
OMW	IntelliCorp				*						W,O,U
Paradigm Plus	Protosoft	*		*	*	*		*		Fusion, other	U/W
Ptech	ADT	*									U,W/O
Rose	Rational	*									W
Select OMT	Select Software					*					U
SES/Objectbench	SES							*			U
Software through Pictures	IDE						*				W
STOOD	TNI			*							W
Synchrony	Easel										W,O
Systems Architect	Popkin		*								M
TurboCASE	Structsoft	*							*		O,U,D
VSF	Virtual Software Facto.								*		U
Westmount OMT	Westmount	*		*							

Platforms: U=Unix; O=OS/2; W=Windows 3; M=Macintosh

Source: Atelier Research, Ovum

Figure 2   CASE Tools: Platform and Method Support

objects. The tools are still implicitly written to support the waterfall life-cycle, assuming a phased approach from analysis to design to implementation. They cannot construct an object data model from existing databases or code (object oriented or not). There needs to be more of a recognition amongst the CASE tool designers of the benefits and advances offered by present and future ADEs. They also are essentially passive, not aiding the analyst or designer in his search for objects to meet the business need, either new or from existing class libraries.

... and Problems of Immaturity
Second, these tools suffer from immaturity: the benefits of CASE given in figure 1 are not actually being achieved today. Compared with existing CASE tools that support structured and data-driven methods, those being used to support object methods are generally not 'industrial strength'. They do not scale well (although in principle they should) and do not have a sufficiently sophisticated approach to supporting concurrent working by team members, for example through managing concurrent access to elements in the design dictionaries. They can, however, link to conventional configuration management tools. In general the tools being used today for object method support are, or are derived from, 'meta-CASE' tools—tools that are configurable to support new or multiple design methods and notations. This gives method support that is wide but not deep: most tools have no great understanding of the semantics of the method and therefore checking of the input information is fairly rudimentary.

Code generation from designs, a major benefit of an integrated CASE product, is so far only rudimentary in tools for object methods, being limited to generation of skeletal pieces of C++ (or, rarely, Smalltalk). There is no generation of (say) peer-to-peer messaging code for distributed system— a main area of promise for object oriented techniques—or of object frameworks or transaction monitor access, as might be found in an ADE. So far, reuse at the specification level is constrained by the lack of such support in the corresponding methods. Long-term, however, reuse of designs and specifications will be facilitated by CASE tool support, giving greater benefit than the code-level reuse offered by programming support systems.

Because of the *potential* of object analysis and design, perseverance with the CASE tool approach is in order. Most of the 'immaturity' shortcomings have been addressed on non-object oriented CASE tools, so it is only a matter of time before they are sorted out for tools for object methods. The integrated approach of the most powerful current CASE tools, based around a central design dictionary, helps with managing large developments, with code generation, and with manipulating systems requirements and production at the specification model level, giving potential quality and productivity benefits.

More robust tools are starting to appear from the CASE 'big names'. The two companies which dominate the technical software development field, Cadre and IDE, have already launched products, but in the business software arena, the only large vendor to show so far is Intersolv, with the latest version of its Excelerator product. This is not a tool with code generation capability, however. We should see more over the next two or three years from companies such as Andersen, LBMS, Oracle and Texas Instruments. (Ironically, these companies are already using object oriented techniques internally, particularly object oriented languages, to build the CASE tools themselves). These companies will squeeze out the smaller tool vendors unless they quickly establish a much bigger market share than at present, based on enhanced functionality and robustness. The large vendors' offerings will of course appeal primarily to their existing user base, and they will tend to support evolutionary approaches.

For long-term investment, (greater than three years, say) users should wait for mature and functional products from stable companies. In the meantime, tools available today are not to be ignored, they can be extremely useful for prototyping the various methods available today, and hybrids of those methods, for use on small projects, and for building up expertise and design libraries for the future.

Hybrid Tools: the Best of Both Worlds?

Some of the problems with CASE tools for objects are already addressed by present day ADEs. For instance, reverse engineering into an object model from database structures is supported by ART*Enterprise. Hitachi's ObjectIQ has an object library manager that assists with documenting objects in such a way that they can be found by others who may be working on different problem types. The iterative approach is better supported. Conversely, as we have seen, CASE tools can offer several benefits that ADEs do not.

There is no deep reason why implementors should not have the best of both worlds, from combined tools. Fortunately at least two companies have recognised this, and it is to be hoped that more will follow their lead. They are Intellicorp, whose ProKappa tool is integrated with its recently introduced OMW tool, which supports OOIE; and Easel, which has built Synchrony, which supports OMT to some extent, as a layer on top of its Enfin product, an application builder based on Smalltalk. The hybrid approach is a metaphor of great promise, which should yield benefits of assembly-style system building with overall top-down approaches to help deal with large systems problems and high-level reuse.

FUTURE DIRECTIONS IN TOOL SUPPORT

Further out than the melding of conventional CASE and ADEs, more advances are to be desired and even expected, but they will take time to appear, for a variety of reasons.

Most important, few tools are yet available to assist with identification of and reuse of objects, and this position is changing only slowly. There is still work needed to identify the best approach intellectually and mechanically towards the problems of the categorisation, identification and retrieval of objects. Some work has been done by academics such as Prieto-Diaz in the US, and in Europe through various ESPRIT and Eureka projects, but these subjects are still research topics. One thing that is needed is something analogous to the Dewey Decimal cataloguing system found in conventional libraries, but agreement on standards will be a long time coming.

Support for other standards is also important, but will lag the standards themselves. Most important will be interoperability standards such as the Object Management Group's common object request broker architecture (CORBA), Microsoft's OLE (Object Linking and Embedding) technology, and the OSF's distributed computing environment (DCE). These standards will facilitate the plug-and-play interoperability referred to earlier, only presently achievable in closed, heterogeneous environments such as the Smalltalk programming system. Tools which can generate code to use standard mechanisms as well as other middleware layers like transaction processing monitors will be very desirable because they remove the need for staff knowledgeable in the business requirements to also possess skills in these very technical areas.

We can expect CASE tools to change quite significantly to reflect the shift in attitude towards seeing software development as a construction task, split into the two parts of object refining and system assembly. CASE tools will ultimately support object reuse at the specification level, with generation from templates composed of object (class) definitions, possibly to fit in with application frameworks such as those being worked upon by Taligent. Automated support for incorporation of existing systems, applications packages and data into new object schema and new systems requirements will come, albeit slowly.

Further out—almost over the horizon—what is ultimately needed is an intelligent assistant for the design team. A system that can propose, from a sketch of the requirement, a solution taken from existing and, where necessary, new components, putting together a working and documented system for trial and refinement. The analysts and designers would be more applications than technical specialists. It can be seen from this paper both how object-orientation is moving in the right direction, and how far it yet has to go.

TO THE USER: GETTING THERE FROM HERE

There is one overriding message from this paper for potential users of object methods and CASE tools: this is an area of great promise, but it is changing fast, in terms of the methods themselves and the tools used to support them. Therefore all purchases and decisions made in the coming months must be seen as tactical. Investments in education and training in object oriented techniques, and tool support for this, will not be wasted and indeed should start today. But, investing large amounts on tools and systems reliant on them could be unwise.

For those who have not yet embarked on an object oriented project at all, there is plenty that can be done. Start now, with an audit of current practices, develop a training plan, establish pilot projects to raise awareness and skill levels. Integration and migration of existing systems, feasibility studies and so on can all be undertaken now and indeed the sooner the better.

To close, a quotation from Bjarne Stroustrup, devisor of the C++ language, is very apt:

'With any new technology there is a risk. If you move too fast you will find yourself ahead of the education and support tools. If you don't move at all, you will find yourself left behind.'

REFERENCES

Adams S and Burbeck S. *Software Assets by Design*. White paper, available from Knowledge Systems Corp., Cary, NC, USA, 1992a.
Adams S. *Object Transition by Design*. White paper, available from Knowledge Systems Corp., Cary, NC, USA, 1992b.
Beck K and Cunningham W. A Laboratory for Teaching Object-Oriented Thinking. *Proceedings OOPSLA*, 1989.

Boehm B. A Spiral Model of Software Development and Enhancement. *IEEE Computer*, **21**(5) 1988.

Booch G. *Object Oriented Design with Applications, 2nd edn*. Benjamin Cummings, 1993.

Bowles A. Visions, Plans, and the Next Lifecycle. *Object Magazine*, **3**(3) September-October 1993.

Coad P and Yourdon E. *Object Oriented Design*, Prentice Hall, 1991.

Coleman D. *Object Oriented Development: The Fusion Method*, Prentice Hall, 1993.

Gibson E. Objects – Born and Bred. *BYTE Magazine*, October 1990.

Goldberg A and Rubin K. *Object Behavior Analysis*. Internal white paper from Parcplace Systems, Inc., Sunnyvale, CA, USA, 1993.

Henderson-Sellers B. *A Book of Object Oriented Knowledge*, Prentice Hall, 1993.

Jacobson I and Christerson M. *Object Oriented Software Engineering: A Use Case Driven Approach*, Addison-Wesley, 1992.

Jeffcoate J and Wesley I. *Objects in Use*. Ovum, London, UK, 1992.

Martin J. *Information Engineering*, Prentice Hall, 1990.

Martin J and Odell J. *Object Oriented Analysis and Design*, Prentice Hall, 1992.

Rumbaugh J *et al*. *Object Oriented Modeling and Design*, Prentice-Hall, 1991.

Sanders P and Short K. Declarative Analysis in Information Engineering, in *CASE—Current Practice, Future Prospects*, Spurr K and Layzell P (eds.). Wiley, 1992.

Shlaer S and Mellor S J. *Object Oriented Systems Analysis: Modeling the World in Data*, Prentice Hall, 1988.

Wirfs-Brock R *et al*. *Designing Object Oriented Software*, Prentice Hall, 1990.

Section 3

Managing the Transition

9

Managing the Move to Object Oriented Development

Nick Whitehead

ABSTRACT

We are at an early stage in the use of object oriented technology. Early adopters are just beginning to derive real benefit on very large projects. Many more have now run their first successful pilot and are moving on to bigger things. Most people are just beginning to consider the move. This paper is for them!

The paper discusses Cadre's experiences using object oriented software development techniques since 1986, and some of the lessons learned. In addition, it proposes some considerations and criteria for the selection of an appropriate method for object oriented development.

CADRE TECHNOLOGIES' EXPERIENCE WITH OBJECT ORIENTED TECHNOLOGY

Cadre Technologies Inc. was founded in 1982 by Lou Mazzucchelli.

Business Objects: Software Solutions. Edited by Kathy Spurr, Paul Layzell, Leslie Jennison and Neil Richards
© 1994 John Wiley & Sons Ltd

Mazzucchelli was at the time working for Ed Yourdon at his consultancy, and tried unsuccessfully to get Ed to develop a tool to automate his structured approach to software development. Mazzucchelli decided to 'go it alone', and with a colleague from Brown University, Providence, Rhode Island they raised some venture capital and set to work.

The rest is history. Best known for the structured analysis and design workbench, Teamwork, in 1994 Cadre have 35,000 systems installed worldwide. Our development language of choice since 1986 has been C++. Now all new development is done in C++, and to date we have approximately 1/4 million lines of C++ shipping in our products. We considered ourselves then—and now—to be on the 'bleeding edge' of technology and learned some useful lessons along the way. For the most part, this paper focuses on these lessons.

Our support for the automation of OO methods focuses on two of the leading commercially tried and tested ones—Shlaer-Mellor OOA/ Recursive Design (Shlaer and Mellor, 1988) and Rumbaugh *et al*.'s (1991) Object Modeling Technique (OMT). The product family is called ObjectTeam. Part of this paper will consider criteria to consider when selecting an OO method.

MOTIVES FOR MOVING TO OBJECT ORIENTED DEVELOPMENT

Steve Cook (1993), of Object Designers, suggests that moving to OO is a paradigm shift in the practice of software development similar (though not of the same magnitude) to that made when cosmologists figured out that the sun—not the earth—was the centre of the universe.

If we are to adopt such a paradigm shift, we had better make sure that we understand our motives for doing so. There are only two motives, as ever, to change our software development process.

- To produce better quality software.

- To do it faster.

Two fundamental promises of OO lead us to think that indeed it can deliver this goal: (i) better architecture, and (ii) reuse. By using an object oriented architecture you can manage complexity by decomposing the subject matter of your problem along more natural lines than that offered by traditional functional decompositions. The types of objects and their relationship to other objects are less likely to change (though each object is equally subject to change as any function ever was). Objects that are stable are good candidates for reuse.

OBJECT ORIENTED REALITY

Cadre learned the hard way that OO is difficult! At least, back in 1986 it was difficult:

- There was not the preponderance of good quality programming tools available as there is today.
- The methods were immature.
- We had little experience to fall back on.
- There were no CASE tools.

OO programming languages provide us with a set of constructs to enable us to build better architectures—classes, inheritance, polymorphism, templates, etc. But constructing good architectures is not easy. Cadre wrote a lot of C++ code in the early days which turned out to be unmaintainable because we did not understand how to use OO concepts like inheritance and polymorphism effectively. Give OO programming constructs to the inexperienced and everything begins to look like a class! Now we are older and wiser and know a little better. More on this later. Another lesson we learned is that using OO does not necessarily lead directly to effective reuse of software components. For a start, without an effective way of classifying and storing reusable components, it is very difficult to find the right component to fit the job.

Finally, the technology to help integrate these OO components into an overall design was poorly understood. Now some really useful standards and technologies are emerging from members of groups like OMG (1990) and ODMG to help in this area.

AN EVOLUTIONARY PERSPECTIVE

When the cosmologists learned that the universe resolved around the sun rather than the earth, although it changed fundamentally their perception of the universe, they did not throw out all they currently knew. The same is true of OO. An evolutionary perspective is required. Retain and use all that we have learned about good software engineering principals as you move forward into OO. Consider OO as the next step in refining the process, turning software development from a craft into a science. Consider carefully how existing legacy systems can be incorporated into ongoing development using OO techniques (more on this later). Above all, remember as developers there are still three fundamental responsibilities:

1.   To thoroughly understand the problem. This should be a two way interaction with the customer to ensure that you and the customer understand exactly what is required of the delivered system. One of the major benefits we have seen from the use of OO over structured methods is the rigor inherent in the approach. All methods deal with three facets of the system—data, control and function. In OO analysis techniques, the relationships between models used to specify these three facets are much more rigorously defined.

2.   To design an appropriate solution. Make sure the solution meets the requirement, is cost effective and is easy to maintain. If you do not achieve this goal, it will directly affect both your bottom line (as profit is eroded both during development and ensuing maintenance) and your relationship with the customer (important if you want to continue to have his custom!).

3.   To implement it well. Use effective technologies during implementation. Choose an appropriate language and platform. Choose the right database if persistent storage of data is important. Define a testing strategy designed to validate implementation against requirements. Document the delivered solution, etc.

DEFINE A DEVELOPMENT PROCESS

In his book *Object Oriented Software Engineering—a Use Case Approach*, Ivar Jacobson (1993) makes the distinction between process and method. Methods tend to focus on specific parts of the development process. Normally analysis and design methods are well defined but managing requirements (traceability), coding, testing and on-going maintenance are not covered. The need for an overall process for software development is far more important. This process should encompass all activities involved in turning requirements into delivered systems.

Remember, tools will not help improve either quality or speed of development unless they are used within a context of a well defined process. When they certainly will! Three points to note about process:

1.   Define work products developed as part of the process, and work out how to generate them from your chosen tool chain.

2.   Make sure you understand how to make the transition between phases. This is very important with OO because the separation of

analysis and design is blurred. Indeed, Steve Mellor of Project Technology Inc. suggests that 'design is a bankrupt concept', and advocates design by translation of analysis models into the implementation 'domain'—called recursive design. In contrast Rumbaugh *et al.* (1991) and Booch (1991) advocate stepwise refinement of analysis models and the addition of implementation detail within the same notational framework as analysis.

3.   Measure the process. Unless you are able to quantify the effect of changing your process you will not be able to make valued judgements about the benefits of modifications.

As you define your process you will be considering which OO method you will use to model the user's requirement and implement it. Some points on models.

•   Analysis models are not the same as requirements. Analysis models are formalised representations of requirements, designed to express requirements in a way which is clear and unambiguous. Analysts use models to help them understand what the user wants. But do not expect the user to understand your models—show a prototype instead.

•   Models help to manage complexity by abstracting what is important about requirements in a formal way. Because requirements are formally represented in an analysis model, they are the starting point for implementation. As decisions about implementation are made further analysis modelling helps you map user requirements into the implementation.

All methods (even OO ones) deal with at least three different viewpoints of the problem domain:

1.   *Data*. What information is managed by the system? In OO methods this is the object model.

2.   *Control*. How does the system react to external events, and promulgate actions and events within the system? In OO this is the behavioural model. There is a behavioural model for each object (with interesting behaviour) in the system.

3.   *Function*. The mechanics of reading events, transforming data and generating actions. There is function associated with each state in the behavioural model of each object in the object model.

The method should define explicitly the relationship between each view. OO is much better at this than structured methods.

WHERE ARE WE WITH OBJECT ORIENTED METHODS?

OO methods are still evolving. If we imagine an analogy of the history of flight, the methods have gone through some early prototypes. Aeroplane design starting with some early ideas—hot air balloons, engines at the front, at the back, in the middle. one wing, two wings, three wings, flying boats, zeppelins, etc. In the 1950s the format of all aircraft stabilised. We are now at the stage were all agree about the basic shape of the method for OO. All methods now deal with the three basic concepts of object models, behavioural models and process models.

Now developments are focused on issues relating to how to proceed to design from analysis. Two fundamentally different approaches are evolving. That of iteration, or round trip gestalt design from the likes of Rumbaugh *et al.* and Booch. And translation, as defined by the ideas behind Recursive Design from Shlaer and Mellor. Other innovations such as Jacobson's 'Use Case' for defining user scenarios are beginning to emerge. In the future, these concepts will be refined, along with new developments aimed at areas such as validation of analysis models through simulation, system construction and assembly, and support for reuse.

At present there are purported to be in excess of 30 published OO approaches. Others will emerge and die. Some will merge with others. For instance, Rumbaugh is embracing Jacobson's concept of Use Case. But some clear leaders are emerging and gaining widespread commercial acceptance. These are the ones that have been tried and tested on real projects.

As in structured methods, developers of methods initially used surface syntax and notation to differentiate their approaches. After a while, people realised that the underlying semantic issues were more important and notations began to converge. Tool providers supported and encouraged this convergence in order to build an economically viable market base for their tools.

Unfortunately the OO methods marketplace differs from the structured methods marketplace in that almost every method developer seems to have their own tool to sell. This makes it harder to evaluate a method or tool on its own merit. It also makes it difficult for standards to emerge because there are so many proprietary interests.

Many more methods and ideas will come and go. Leaders will evolve and take on new and innovative concepts. But beware the new plane maker with a new and (so they say) better concept. There is considerable risk involved in taking on board a new and untried concept.

Ask yourself the following questions:

- What are the business drivers for improving the development process?

- What specific benefits are derived from using a particular method or tool?

- What can be represented in method A that cannot be represented in method B?

- Why is that useful?

- How can early benefits be achieved?

- How do I communicate and share information with users of other tools and methods?

- What is the method or tool vendor doing to incorporate the work of others and drive towards industry standards?

Rumbaugh *et al.* (1991) make the observation 'All the object oriented methodologies, including ours, have much in common and should be contrasted more with non-OO methodologies than with each other.'

SO WHICH METHOD?

OO methods, like structured methods, should be chosen on the basis of their focus. Some methods are more appropriate to a particular type of problem domain or organisational culture. Below is a list of factors you should consider when making your choice.

Apart from focus, consider method maturity and popularity. This has some interesting side effects. Since you are likely to need external help in taking on board new ideas, you should consider whether training is available, and whether you will be able to recruit staff.

Ask yourself the following questions:

- How many commercial training organisations teach it?

- How much does it cost?

- How specific is it?

- How up to date is it? Methods are still evolving.

- Will it be there in two years time?

- How easy is it to recruit? Is there a body of trained practitioners out there?

- Am I offering a dead end? Will employees be enthusiastic about learning new techniques which will not be valuable to them in terms of career development?

The most useful technique we have found when advising customers which of the methods we support is the most appropriate is to profile their project and development culture. We can imagine two projects at different ends of the spectrum, and some of their characteristics (Figure 1).

On the left-hand side of Figure 1 are some of the characteristics of development in the technical sector. Projects are big and last many years and involve hundreds of developers working on different part of the system in parallel. Take a satellite control system. You must meet the

Project A	Project B
Long development lifecycle	Relatively short, multiple release development life-cycle
Large project split into smaller groups	Single focused project
Multiple development groups	Single development group
Formal project deliverables	Analysis and design are a means to an end
Product delivery is the main	Product time to market is main objective
Quality is pre-requisite	Quality is a desireable aspect
Code reuse is relatively minor	Code reuse is a commercial necessity
Tools should be stable	Tools should be flexible in method support

Figure 1   Project Profiles

customer's requirement in the first release, because quite possibly there is only one release. Quality is tantamount. If the satellite fails there is no opportunity to fix it.

On the right-hand side of Figure 1 are some characteristics of commercial development. Here, teams are smaller and it is likely that the analyst is also the designer and programmer. Commercial pressures mean using of the shelf commercial software is a necessity. Time to market is all important—if the release is late it impacts directly your ability to be profitable because your competitive advantage is eroded. Of course, quality is important, but if errors are evident you have the opportunity to fix them in the next release.

Cadre support two methods—Shlaer Mellor OOA/Recursive Design and Rumbaugh *et al.*'s OMT. We advocate the use of OMT for commercial projects because of its iterative approach and the expressive power of the notation, and OOA/Recursive Design for technical projects because of the rigor of the method and the well defined audit path from analysis to implementation through the translation of analysis models. Of course it is not a simple as that, but it is a good place to start!

MAKE-A-METHOD?

Many organisations consider developing their own method which will be tuned specifically to their own organisation and culture.

Beware! Ask yourself whether the new approach is unique and deals with any concept which is particular to your organisation. If it does, fine! But understand the implications of using your own approach. The cost of developing your own method and supporting it can be very high. Many of the costs tend to be hidden.

There are costs associated with the following issues:

- Developing your own tools—and supporting them yourself.

- Training new recruits, because you will not be able to hire staff with skills in your proprietary method.

- Dealing with problems with the new proprietary method as they arise. With public domain methods many of the problems will have been ironed out and there will be a body of published work detailing experiences with the method.

- Selling your own approach to management within the organisation, and more importantly to customers who would rather see you use a tried and tested method—perceived to be a less risky option.

Remember, there is scope to add your own particular features to an existing method to make it more applicable to your own development culture. And off the shelf tools are increasingly able to accommodate this type of tailoring. You are probably better off investing your efforts in this direction than building your own from scratch.

TOOL SUPPORT FOR OBJECT ORIENTED DEVELOPMENT

Since a major focus in software development is the delivery of the real benefit of advanced productivity, automation of methods takes on some added importance. Added to that, concepts like inheritance and polymorphism can be much harder to design directly in C++ than C, even though (and perhaps because) C++ is more compact. We have found that understanding the underlying functionality and design intent of a random page of undocumented C++ source code is non-trivial. Figure 2 shows some figures published by Bellcore in *Software* magazine (July 1993) which correspond to our early experience indicating that as you move to OO, there will be a greater emphasis on analysis and design than with structured approaches.

When we first started looking at OO development, we quickly learned that graphical design representations of OO programs were extremely

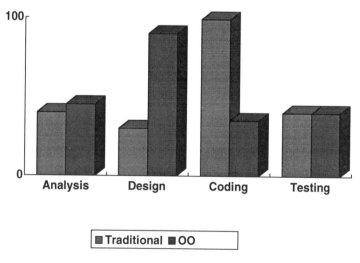

Figure 2   Change of Emphasis Away from Code (Source: *Software Magazine*, Bellcore, July 1993)

useful because they allowed designers to focus on architecture, rather than implementation issues. Code alone is not sufficient. We set about 'bootstrapping' an OO tool, using object oriented techniques, from our existing structured toolset. We started by using our Ada design editor which supported an extended Buhr notation (Buhr, 1984), and added other facilities to support additional concepts and language constructs developed by Cadre and Project Technologies Inc. in a notation called OODLE (Object Oriented Design LanguagE) (Hecht *et al.,*). We developed a tool to help create and manage all OODLE diagram types and provide navigation between views with simple point-and-click operations. We also added design rule checkers for consistency and tools to generate C++ source code from OODLE models.

While this design support helped us (and our customers) ensure a good implementation, it is still necessary to understand the problem before you begin to design a solution. So we set about providing support for Shlaer and Mellor's analysis formalism—OOA (Shlaer and Mellor, 1989). Most of the lessons reported in this paper reflect our experience during this early work. Using these graphical abstractions and method semantics without the aid of automated tools is not practical. So considering the level of tool support when choosing a method is important.

The figures in Figure 3 are based on a 'straw poll' conducted at

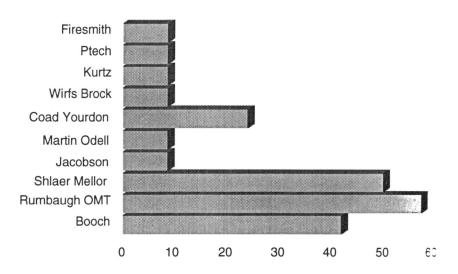

Figure 3   Percentage of Number of Tools Surveyed at ObjectExpo 1993

ObjectExpo, London in 1993. They represent the percentage of methods supported by the tools on show. So, for instance, over half of the tools supported the OMT method from Rumbaugh *et al*.

GET MANAGEMENT BUY-IN

It is as important for managers as it is for technologists to understand the implications of a fundamental change in the software development process.

Managers should understand the new process, so that they can make any appropriate management or organisational changes. For instance, organisational change will be necessary to gain maximum benefit from reuse. The way in which design walk-throughs and reviews are conducted will change. Concepts like Shlaer Mellor's Recursive Design fundamentally change the transition from analysis to design.

Clearly such changes are designed to benefit the process by improving quality and efficiency. But how? And exactly what? What are the objectives? What are the risks? How are developers going to deal with existing legacy systems as they move to OO? If managers are not aware of the potential pitfalls, they cannot hope to manage their way round them. Above all, managers should be totally committed to making the changes successful.

DESIGNING FOR MAINTAINABILITY

System maintainability is a function of good development practice, both with traditional approaches, and with OO approaches.

Central to building easily maintained systems using OO programming constructs is the development of a good architecture. Use OO programming concepts with care, and ensure you adhere to good software engineering principles. In the early days Cadre threw out lots of C++ code as we grappled with new and unfamiliar OO concepts because it contained impossibly convoluted inheritance trees.

You should consider at least two views of the system:

- Class design, which focuses on inheritance relationships, reference relationships and dependencies.

- Method design which deals with method interfaces and modularity issues.

Traditional concepts from structured design (Yourdon and Constantine, 1978) may be applied to methods and classes. Coupling can be thought of as the knowledge one class has of another—the designer's goal is to minimise coupling to increase class independence. Cohesion is a measure of the conceptual integrity of a class—the designer's goal is to maximise cohesion to ensure localisation of functions, thereby reducing the maintenance effort.

Of course, there are often good reasons for violating these general rules in specific instances, perhaps to improve the efficiency of the code. But is is important that if code is modified in this way, then the design views (from which documentation is derived) should be updated to reflect the change. Tools which reverse engineer design views from source code can automate this process. It is good practice to incrementally reverse engineer code every time you begin to build a new release. In this way you can be sure that the design view *exactly* represents the code shipped.

INVEST IN CONFIGURATION AND BUILD MANAGEMENT

Block structured languages like C have a very simple architecture—a call hierarchy. OO languages present an architecture which is inherently client-server. Classes are self contained units of code that manage data and perform functions based simply a defined set of events (or inputs). Consequently, working out which classes use other classes and how to make sure that all the necessary classes (and the right versions) are included in a build can be challenging.

The nature of OO development encourages a highly iterative approach, with much prototyping. In such a culture, there is likely to be lots of work products developed—models, code, test plans, etc. Keeping track of what versions are what, and what ends up in the delivered system demands careful control. Cadre have invested heavily in this aspect of our process, and have purchased tools specifically to help configure and manage multiple versions of all the work products (code, models, requirements, test specifications, etc.) produced during development.

To gain the maximum benefit from reuse, a well developed set of reusable components needs to be defined and managed. Make sure someone in the organisation has specific responsibility for managing the reuseable components, and that a specific person within the organisation has responsibility for its design, maintenance, quality (testing) and documentation.

FOCUS ON DESIGN EARLY

Stepping back from the design problem, we found that regardless of whether or not one uses OO technology, a solution must satisfy some key constraints:

- Meets the functional requirements.

- Fits the run time constraints.

- Can be developed within resource budget (People, time, space, material).

- Designed with appropriate longevity in mind.

To achieve this goal we need to think about the problem in a language independent fashion at a higher level of abstraction than C++ constructs. Thus we had strong incentives to focus on the design issues. Simply stated, design is the process of transforming 'what' (a statement of requirements) into 'how' (an implementation). The design process is supposed to help us deal with complexity as we make this transformation.

OO design approaches promise faster development more reuse and smaller, more maintainable implementations. While these promises can be realised, it will not be because we have sprinkled 'OO magic dust' on the problem. It will be because we have applied good design sense to realise these benefits.

THE INHERITANCE TRAP

Inheritance is a very powerful concept. Cadre use it extensively but from experience we now use it wisely.

Remember, using inheritance will tend to scatter functions among parents and children within a hierarchy. And there is no specific way to identify exactly where a particular function is either described or implemented. Its use also tends to introduce dependencies between members of the same hierarchy—class, subclass and superclass—which are difficult to visualise or comprehend. Abstracted design views captured in a CASE tool, coupled with the 'point-and-click' capabilities they provide to navigate through the hierarchy can help here.

There is a tendency for OO programmers to use inheritance to produce a subclass to do a particular job from another which nearly does the job. 'Just make a subclass' is not a good answer to many problems.

Remember, maintainability of the system will be directly related to the number of dependencies between classes and methods. So make sure you concentrate on software design principles like low coupling and high cohesion.

BENEFITTING FROM REUSE

One of the prime motivators for moving to OO is the promise of significant benefit from reuse. It is true that using OO may result in the development of some stable components for reuse. But just using OO does not guarantee success. Reuse is a cultural issue!

Software development is essentially a creative exercise, so using the fruits of other people's effort is not considered fulfilling. In addition, because finding the right component for reuse without a well defined taxonomy for categorising and storing reuseable components is difficult, it is often considered easier to build from scratch than to find the right component. Organisations must measure the benefit of reduced maintenance from using an existing component against the extra work done up front in finding it and integrating it into a design.

Reuse must be culturally acceptable within an organisation. Developers should get kudos from using a suitable existing component in place of developing their own. Make a specific level of reuse a company and project goal.

Some observations on Cadre's experience in developing reusable components:

- Focus on classes for your application. Benefits can be gained from identifying reusable aspects of your organisation's areas of key competency. Not only reuseable classes but also whole reusable domains—user interface, archiving, device management, etc.

- Attempting to identify reusable components up front is not always productive. Instead, let the general purpose evolve from the special purpose. Use an object oriented approach to build an application, then identify key areas which will be useful for future development as candidates for reuse.

- Having identified these reusable components, make sure that they are well documented and tested. Users will have much more confidence in using an off the shelf component if they understand the task it is supposed to do, and have confidence that it will work.

DEALING WITH LEGACY SYSTEMS

Two issues arise: (i) how to deal with existing databases; and (ii) how to combine legacy code during the transistion.

Mapping relational databases onto new object oriented applications is well documented by Rumbaugh *et al*. (1991). Much is published about the so called 'impedance mismatch' between the relational table model for storing data and the hierarchical model supported by object oriented methods. While using a true OO database management system does away with the impedance mismatch, commercial expediency and the advantages of using tried and tested technology indicates that the relational systems will remain the norm. Commercial systems are available which map object oriented programs onto relational data models, and deal with the complexity of implementing OO data modelling concepts such as inheritance which are not supported by the relational model.

A two stage approach to combining legacy code with new OO development is recommended. Initially it may be possible to call the legacy C code from within the classes of the new system (for instance, call C from C++). This will allow immediate access to legacy code in the new system. For code that is required for long term reuse, encapsulation of functionality into classes in the new system is the answer. Again, tools can automate part of this, by reverse engineering data and function declarations into the repository as candidate attributes and methods which can then be 'shrink wrapped' into new class declarations, and regenerated in the new code.

THE IMPORTANCE OF TRAINING

Training is an important part of any technology adoption program. There are many new and powerful concepts to take on board. Do not make the mistake of thinking C++ is just a superset of C and expect all your experienced C programmers to pick up and use concepts like polymorphism without training.

A training program should be well thought out and implemented. Most importantly, do not expect to train the whole team en masse and all at once. Different roles will require different skill sets. And they do not necessarily need to know it all at once. Do training 'just in time'. Learn a particular set of skills and put it into practice straight away. Even a gap of a few weeks between learning and practising is detrimental. Choose a training organisation who can be flexible in their approach, and ask them to tailor their courses and offerings to suite your project and timescales.

Two further points:

- consider a 'train the trainers' approach

- do not forget to train the managers. If they do not understand the new process, how can they hope to manage it?

THE IMPORTANCE OF GOOD PROGRAM ARCHITECTURE

Getting a good design architecture is key to success. Think carefully about implementation techniques early in the design process. If you need to use a persistence storage mechanism, which type? Will your application work stand-alone on a single computer, or do you need to go multi-processor or client server? What will the interconnection technology be? How will you map analysis concepts into design and implementation? Will your chosen architecture meet your performance constraints?

Make these decisions the responsibility of your most experienced OO developer. And when you have an architecture prototype parts of your system to make sure it will meet your customer's requirements and constraints.

Managers must expect to take time in the early development of the system architecture before code that meets user requirements can be observed. Use of prototyping of areas key to meeting the customer's requirement can help here. Practice these new techniques and try out the new process on a pilot study. Usual rules for technology insertion apply:

- Try and choose an area well suited to OO. We chose our user interface and more recently our methodology meta models.

- Make sure it is off the critical path. You are certain to meet unforeseen problems, and pressures to meet timescales will detract from your ability to gain benefit from the pilot.

- Consider and define your motives for changing the process. Identify clear and tangible objectives and goals.

- Measure the new process and compare with results from previous work. When complete, consider have you improved quality? Have you improved efficiency? Remember also that the benefits of reuse will not be realised until the second or subsequent times around.

- Gain clear support from the entire team, especially managers.

CONCLUSIONS

Remember, OO is not some panacea or 'magic dust' which will make all your software development problems vanish. All the usual software development activities still need to be done:

- Understand the problem.

- Design an appropriate solution.

- Implement it well.

The usual rules for project management still apply—especially configuration and build management.

Remember that as with anything new, you can expect to make some mistakes and identify unforeseen circumstances in the early stages. So do a pilot before betting the company, or your job, on the new approach.

REFERENCES

Booch G. *Object Oriented Design with Applications*, Benjamin-Cummings, CA, 1991.

Buhr R J A. *System Design with Ada*, Prentice Hall, NJ, 1984.

Cook S. Analyisis, Design, Programming: What's the Difference? *Proceedings TaTTOO '94—teaching and training in the technology of objects*, Leicester, UK, 1994.

Hecht A, Shlaer S, Mellor S J and Hywari W. *Teamwork Support for OODLE: A Language Independent Notation for Object oriented design*. Cadre Technologies, RI, USA.

Jacobson I *Object Oriented Software Engineering—A Use Case Approach*, Addison Wesley, Wokingham, UK, 1993.

Object Management Architecture Guide, OMG, MA, USA, 1990.

Rumbaugh J *et al*. Object Oriented Modeling and Design, Prentice Hall, NJ, 1991.

Shlaer S and Mellor S. *Object Oriented Systems Analysis: Modelling the world in Data*, Yourdon Press, NJ, 1988.

Shlaer, S and Mellor S. Understanding Object Oriented Analysis. *Hewlett Packard Design Center Magazine*, January 1989.

Shlaer S and Mellor S. *Object Lifecycles. Modeling the World in States*, Yourdon Press, NJ, 1992.

Yourdon E and Constantine L. *Structured Design*, Yourdon Press, 1978.

FURTHER READING

Wybolt N. Experiences with C and Object Oriented Software Development. *ACM Software Engineering Notes* **15**(2), 1990.

Mazzucchelli L. Holding onto What Really Matters, An Evolutionary Perspective on OO, *Object Magazine*, November-December 1992.

Flemming R. Will Computer Aided Software Engineering Come of Age in the 1990s? *Electronic Design*, January 1991.

10

The Impact of Object Technology and OMG Standards on Software Development

Eric Leach

ABSTRACT

Object technology generally, and The Object Management Group's (OMG) standards specifically, are likely to have a major impact on software development and the whole of the software industry during the next ten years. Developments in object technology hold out the prospect of the creation of a component-based software industry, in which applications are assembled from components from many sources; which can be deployed on multiple platforms; and can inter-operate with other components and applications in a heterogeneous operating environment.

This paper presents a view on what this impact is likely to be and draws upon empirical research surveys carried on in the USA and the UK

Business Objects: Software Solutions. Edited by Kathy Spurr, Paul Layzell, Leslie Jennison and Neil Richards
© 1994 John Wiley & Sons Ltd

in 1993 and 1994, and on current OMG Task Force, SIG, Sub-Committee and technical standards' developments and literature. Survey analysis and expert opinion of the impact of object technology on CASE is also presented. Also described is OMG's *modus operandi*, achievements and its future agenda.

INTRODUCTION

Object technology is set to bring about a fundamental change to the way we develop, use, re-use, distribute, deploy and maintain computer software.

Object technology is a set of ideas or principles, rather than software or a methodology. An object is something that has a well defined boundary. Object technology insulates the user (or the program) at its most fundamental level from the details of how things are implemented and allows the user to focus on the things (objects) themselves and the tasks the user wants to accomplish with them. Objects can be documents and files, but also literally anything else, including folders, services, pictures, etc.

The Significance of OMG

For the full benefits of object technology to be realised, there must be one set of object technology standards. One set of standards is something that has not been achieved before in the computer industry.

The OMG, formed in 1989, has made remarkable progress in a relatively short period of time in gaining wide consensus in the formulation of object technology standards. Without denying in any way the work of other IT standards groups, in the object technology domain the OMG's achievements and work in progress are of great significance worldwide, and hence are the subject of a major portion of this paper.

The Object Technology Market

To give the reader some idea of the size of the object technology market, I refer to *Object Technology: Suppliers, Products and Markets* (Jeffcoate *et al.*, 1992). The report identifies and profiles 191 suppliers involved in object technology. The products and services on offer break down into the categories of languages, toolkits, OODBMS, CASE tools and services (especially training). The report predicts that the total revenues from object technology products will grow to $4 billion by 1997. Revenues for object oriented CASE tools are predicted to grow to $304 million by 1997.

Datapro Information Services Group estimated, in November 1993, that the object technology market will grow 67% annually to become a $4 billion market by the end of 1997.

During 1993 and 1994, OMG and Object World Expositions (an OMG and IDG joint venture company) commissioned four pieces of object technology research: Visitors to 1993 Object World events were interviewed in Boston in February (FMS Corp., 1993a), in San Francisco in June (FMS Corp., 1993b) and in London in October (Harries and O'Callaghan, 1994). Also, the largest ever object technology research study was carried out in the USA by OMG and Techvantage Inc. and the research was published in July 1993 (OMG and Techavantage, 1993). In January 1994, visitors to Object World Boston were interviewed, and the research was to be published in April 1994 (Marketing Perspectives, Inc., 1994).

OMG/ TECHVANTAGE RESEARCH STUDY

This section of the paper presents some of the findings of the OMG/ Techvantage research carried out in 1993. A detailed 17 page questionnaire on object technology was completed in early 1993 by 198 IT professionals and 23 object technology experts throughout the USA. The data collected was subjected to intensive statistical examination, using both bivariate (cross tabular) and multivariate (regression and correlation) technologies.

Overall, the study revealed that the outlook for object technology is very positive. Object technology may, indeed, drive the controversial paradigm shift and change the nature of the software industry (see Figure 1). The software vendor structure may need to change, and the professional services market should expect a new service category—object integrators. These integrators will assemble different objects, from multiple vendors, into applications.

On the software distribution front, a new channel may emerge—the object warehouse—which would distribute objects from many vendors. However, software prices are not expected to decrease as a result of object technology adoption. Vendors are blamed by both the majority of IT professionals and object technology experts for the slow adoption of object technology, and vendors are urged to communicate more effectively. Most IT professionals said that by the turn of the century the majority of US companies will use object technology. 1996 was predicted to be the

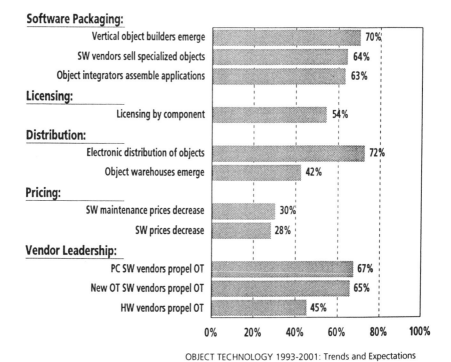

Software Packaging:

OBJECT TECHNOLOGY 1993-2001: Trends and Expectations

Figure 1   Perceived Impact of Object Technology on the Software Industry

'breakout year' for object technology by two-thirds of the experts and a quarter of IT professionals.

Languages, DBMSs and CASE tools were all identified as probable object technology 'drivers'. More than half of the IT professionals believed that current object technology programming languages are too difficult to use, but they are not sure that 4th and 5th generation languages will be any better.

According to IT professionals, object oriented database management systems will co-exist with current relational database management systems, not replace them.

There was no consensus among IT professionals about the future of CASE tools. The majority of professionals agreed with both these statements:

- A new generation of Application Development tools will emerge to replace CASE tools.

- CASE tools will be revitalised with the addition of object technology capabilities and will enjoy a new growth stage.

Editorial note: The wording of the first statement may have contributed to the lack of consensus by making an unnecessary distinction between a new generation of application development tools (which will be CASE tools) and (the current generation of) CASE tools.

Object Technology Adoption Pace—Evolution or Revolution?

Some IT professionals said that object technology adoption will be 'absolutely evolutionary' because it's a 'whole paradigm shift'. Companies don't have the financial resources to make an immediate, total investment in object technology. Additionally, such an investment would place too many mainstream jobs in jeopardy. Most of the experts agreed that the expected timeframe for this evolution is 10 to 20 years.

Some felt it would be revolutionary change, in which evidence of object technology environments will occur as early as 1995, with incremental adoption occuring over the next 10 years. A major catalyst for this shift is the desire of CEOs to lessen dependency on mainframes in favour of a client/server environment.

However, most experts agreed that although the adoption rate may be evolutionary, object technology itself represents a revolution in technology: a move to ubiquitous computing with the availability of information, as well as the process behind this availability, relatively transparent to the average user.

The shift toward giving the end user control over application development, if and when object technology makes this a reality, will truly be revolutionary. Still, the progress in this direction is viewed as gradual and, thus, evolutionary.

Executive management views information systems as a strategic competitive weapon, and they are demanding better solutions. The delivery of faster applications at a lower cost is paramount, as is enabling functional managers to have easy access to information. To this end, MIS departments are seeking alternative solutions, and vendors are seeking to respond with these solutions. Experts viewed object technology as the technology—the means—to address these issues.

To solve business problems, the people who make business decisions must have instantaneous access to the necessary information. Because object technology delivers 'functionality logically', end users will be able to develop their own applications without the rigorous demands of traditional approaches.

Object technology enables companies to assemble the best possible solution through purchasing components from different vendors. This approach will protect a company from being 'stuck' with one vendor who, over time, may not have the newest or best offering.

Several cited the 'infamous application backlog' as a key consideration that will drive object technology adoption. Software development cycles take too long and object technology, specifically distributed object technology, adresses this problem by allowing customers to buy plug-compatible components or modules. Buying these 'smaller chunks' of software will speed up the flow of technology to the user by reducing development time and costs.

Current solutions are unable to easily address technological challenges, such as moving from one operating system or hardware platform to another; connecting multiple platforms within a networked environment; and more complex application requirements. Therefore, many experts believe that object technology is the one approach that will enable these technology problems to be addressed.

As a result of trying to maintain too many 'hardware islands'—such as Sun, Mac, IBM, etc.—companies are experiencing an inability to access and provide data quickly and easily across their diverse platforms. They need to be able to have enhanced heterogeneity in their networks, both on the workstation side and the services side. Object technology provides the mechanism to encapsulate these islands and achieve interoperability.

At the same time, information users must have a range of applications at their fingertips as well as the ability to access and use data from a variety of databases. Object technology enables transparent access through its encapsulation capabilities.

Object technology capabilities are viewed as facilitating the re-engineering of a company's legacy applications and enabling movement to a client/server environment.

Most importantly, object technology fosters a simplified means of developing graphical user interfaces in an event-driven environment. Object technology lets the developer 'hide' the way the GUI is achieved. These GUI capabilities have been initial motivators for object technology adoption and will continue to play an important role in its evolution.

The ability to distribute applications across multiple platforms will be realised, because object technology enables applications to be divided up functionally and incrementally.

Object technology lends itself to manipulating more complex data for applications that make use of multimedia, graphics, and imaging technologies. As a result, these technologies will become more prevalent.

In that same vein, object technology will foster the adoption of parallel procesing because object technology serves as a foundation for building the structure of these processes.

OMG/Techvantage Research Study — Form of Object Technology Adoption

The form of adoption for object technology and how it is introduced into a company will vary among organisations. This will depend both on how object technology is applied, and who in the organisation makes use of it.

Many feel it will be a gradual movement. The slow adopters may purchase applictions that contain object technology. If they decide they like object technology, they will adopt certain object technology tools and integrate them with existing methodologies.

Some experts say object technology will be adopted 'under the covers' of each vendor's software products. As a result, over the next five years, object technology will be so pervasive that it will not even be a 'bullet in list of features' nor a competitive advantage.

Some experts say that the packaged-applications world will give way to a components industry, whereby applications are snapped together using a variety of objects from multiple vendors for the same application.

Other experts say that only the most leading-edge industries (e.g finance) will make a strategic commitment to object technology as a formal structure/methodology. The need to downsize will force the development of in-house applications that use some object technology components, resulting in a gradual mix of object technology and other products.

The most dramatic impact of object technology on the business environment is based on whether end users will begin to develop their own applications by 'snapping' together different objects to form an application.

Some say that object technology is 'ideal' for this environment, because it does not force users to design an application from beginning to end before starting the actual development process. Instead, users can build incrementally or 'on the fly'. Object technology also facilitates and encourages application customisation. This is ideal for the end user, because they 'don't have to have the discipline or education to develop an application as required in today's world.'

A few experts predict that colleges will begin training such 'hybrid' positions as 'domain experts'; professionals who know the problem of particular vertical industries as well as the process of application development. These individuals will be trained in the assembly of vertical components.

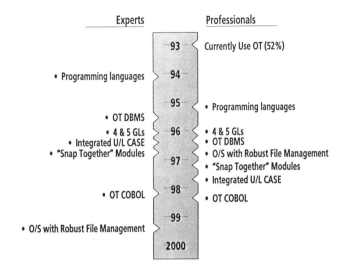

OBJECT TECHNOLOGY 1993-2001: Trends and Expectations

Figure 2   Timeline for Availability of Object Technology Software Products

Object technology could have significant impact on existing product categories, because it enables certain market niches to become more robust and others to revitalize their reputation. Still other market niches will diminish in importance. Thus, object technology will play a significant role in forcing software vendors to re-position their software products and the way they are marketed.

The sequence and timeframe of each product category's adoption will ultimately determine object technology's fate, since most experts agree that available solutions are too rudimentary at this time (see Figure 2).

Some say that object technology will arrive in the form of a new operating system within three years. This operating system will not only include standard operating environment capabilities but will also have enhanced file-server functionality. The need for database systems could be diminished.

Experts disagreed on the impact that object technology will have on languages, and *vice versa*. One opinion is that languages such as C++ (and to a lesser extent Smalltalk) will inhibit object technology adoption because of their complexity

However, the opposing view is that C+ + is 'very forgiving' in its syntax and portability, and it will be the dominant language over the next five years.

Other experts say that the advent of object technology fourth and fifth-generation languages are needed to propel object technology adoption. They predict availability in 3–5 years. Still others indicate that the availability of an object technology COBOL (in 2–3 years) is critical for success.

It was also proposed that the problems of existing object technology languages can be displaced by the evolution to a semantic engine language.

Some experts believe that CASE technology was delivered too early, with inadequate product capabilities and underdeveloped market need and receptivity. However, several feel that a 'marriage' betwen CASE and object technology may provide the foundation that CASE needs to make a successful comeback. Although this marriage is considered 'feasible'—as evidenced by the usage of object technology in enhanced tools—it hasn't occurred yet. Others predict that object technology will replace CASE.

The scalability of development tools is a significant weakness on the part of object technology. Many predict availability of simple tools in 1–3 years, with delivery of a more sophisticated toolset available in five years. The object technology infrastructure will enable the integration of upper and lower CASE tools to establish a new category of integrated—design, analysis, implementation—software solutions in 5–7 years.

Error diagnosis and management must also be addressed, with an emphasis on tools that enable re-usability. Respondents feel that the tool/components market needs to mature. Right now, the tools are geared for 'object geeks'. This focus needs to be turned around, so that the tools are more business-oriented as opposed to 'techie-oriented'.

IT professionals were asked when they believed object technology would become a pervasive technology, both in their own companies and in all US businesses.

Despite the fact that half of them see object technology as developing too slowly, half of them also see the technology as being used by at least 50% of all US companies by 1998, and by nearly 80% of US companies by the turn of the century.

Their projections may be a bit optimistic. Through 1995, IT professionals see other companies adopting object technology at a faster rate than their own companies. By the breakout year however, these professionals see their own companies adopting object technology at a faster rate than the average of all US companies (see Figure 3).

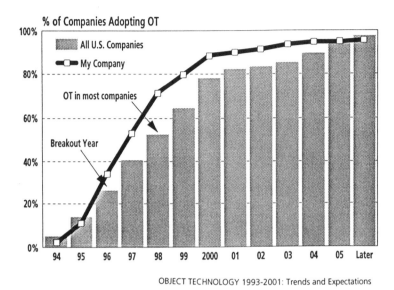

OBJECT TECHNOLOGY 1993-2001: Trends and Expectations

Figure 3   Timescale for Object Technology Adoption

OBJECT WORLD RESEARCH STUDIES

The Object World series of object technology exhibitions and conferences is well established in the USA (east and west coast), Japan, Germany, Australia and the UK. Visitors were interviewed at events in Boston (February 1993 and January 1994), San Francisco (June 1993) and in London (October 1993).

The most recently fully analysed survey results are the views of visitors to Object World UK held at the Ramada Heathrow Hotel 13–15 October, 1993. It is the analysis of these visitors' views that we will concentrate on in this paper.

When presented with possible choices for 'The primary reason' for their move to object technology respondents typically chose more than one. Responses came from 156 respondents. In descending order, their choices were as shown in Figure 4.

Again, comparison with the US is useful. In the San Francisco survey the question was phrased and presented in a slightly different way, but there is some mileage in comparing the order in which the factors are

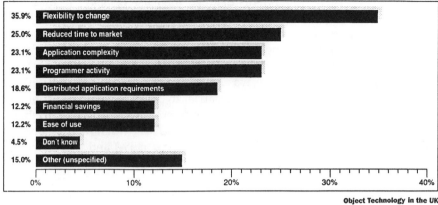

Object Technology in the UK
Object World Expositions

Figure 4   Main Reasons for Moving to Object Technology

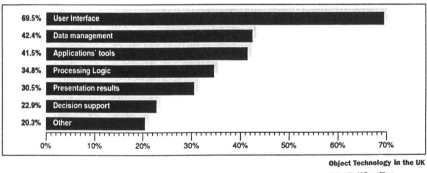

Object Technology in the UK
Object World Expositions

Figure 5   Use of Object Technology Components in Current Applications

ranked. In the US, 'Programmer productivity' proved to be the most popular reason for change, followed by 'Distributed application interoperability' and 'Ease of use'. At Object World Boston in January 1994, however, 'Reduced time to market' followed by 'Increased software re-use" were elected as the top two reasons for moving to object technology.

The strong showing of 'Flexibility to change' again in the UK in this question, does suggest a significant difference between the British and US markets.

Object World UK respondents detailed their use of object technology and the results were as shown in Figure 5.

Again, these results seem to be in the same area as the results of a similar question put to attendees of Object World in San Francisco, excepting a slightly higher use in 'Applications' tools' in the US than in the UK.

'Organisational acceptance' was identified by twice as many Object World UK respondents as any other barrier to object technology adoption (see Figure 6). In fact, nearly half of the answers (44%) included it in their list. Other factors indicated were 'Lack of standards' (identified by one in five) and 'Training' (14.6%). The 'Lack of Tools' (13%) and 'Problems of interoperability' (12%) were also mentioned, while 18% indicated there were 'Other' barriers which they did not specify.

In the Object World San Francisco survey 'Organisational acceptance' was also the top-ranking factor without being so dominant and the 'Lack of training' came next. The 'Lack of standards' fell much further down the list of perceived barriers than it did in the UK—possibly reflecting the stronger base of the OMG in the US to date.

OBJECT MANAGEMENT GROUP

In May 1989, eight companies founded an organisation dedicated to fostering the development and growth of object oriented software development. These companies were 3Com Corporation, American Airlines, Canon,Inc., Data General, Hewlett-Packard, Philips Telecommunications N.V., Sun Microsystems and Unisys Corporation. The organisation they

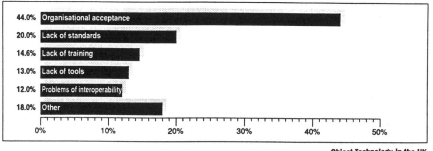

Object Technology in the UK
Object World Expositions

Figure 6   Perceived Barriers to Object Technology Adoption

formed is The Object Management Group (OMG). OMG is the prime driving force in the world of object technology and is an international organisation supported by over 380 information system vendors, software developers, consultants and users. The organisation's charter includes the establishment of industry guidelines and object management specifications to provide a common framework for application development. Conformance to these specifications will make it possible to develop a heterogeneous applications environment across all major hardware platforms and operating systems.

The OMG defines object management as software development that models the real world through the representation of 'objects'. These objects are the encapsulation of the attributes, relationships and methods of software identifiable program components. A key benefit of an object oriented system is its ability to expand in functionality by extending existing components and adding new objects to the system. Object management results in faster application development, easier maintenance and reusable software. The acceptance and use of object technology is widespread and growing.

OMG 's Standards Agenda

The objectives of the OMG are to foster the technology's growth and influence its direction in the following four areas:

1. *Overall Architecture, Reference Model and Terms*
   Industry-wide consensus on an Object Management Architecture (OMA) which includes the definition of terms and a common model for objects and their attributes, relationships and methods.

2. *Applications Programming Interfaces (APIs) for Objects and Applications*
   Object management facilities for a common API across all operating systems, including distribution, class libraries, document content architectures and methodolology.

3. *Distributed Object Management*
   Applications and APIs for the distribution of objects across heterogeneous networks, remote procedure calls (RPCs) and operating systems.

4. *Object Services*
   Specifications for interfaces and common services, such as data management, linking and transactions, security authentication and system management.

OMG upgraded and reissued its Object Management Architecture (OMA) Guide in 1992 (Soley, 1992). This guide contains OMG's Reference Model which is the central design guideline OMG uses for the creation of a distributed object computing environment (see Figure 7). OMG's Reference Model is OMG's conceptual roadmap to be followed to achieve OMG's technical standards' goals. The model has four main components—Object Request Broker, Common Facilities, Object Services and Application Services.

One of the key components of the OMA is the OMG Object Model. The Object Model is used by all OMG-compliant technologies such as The Common Object Request Broker: Architecture and Specification (CORBA).

This model defines a common object semantics for specifying the externally visible characteristics of objects in a standard and implementation-independent way. The common semantics characterise objects that exist in an OMG-compliant system. These systems perform operations and maintain state for objects.

The externally visible characteristics of objects are described by an interface which consists of operation signatures. The external view of both object behaviour and object state (information needed to alter the outcome of a subsequent operation) are modelled in terms of operation signatures.

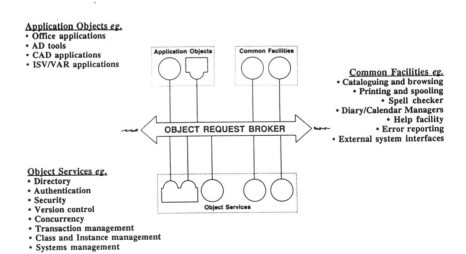

Application Objects *eg.*
* Office applications
* AD tools
* CAD applications
* ISV/VAR applications

Common Facilities *eg.*
* Cataloguing and browsing
* Printing and spooling
* Spell checker
* Diary/Calendar Managers
* Help facility
* Error reporting
* External system interfaces

Object Services *eg.*
* Directory
* Authentication
* Security
* Version control
* Concurrency
* Transaction management
* Class and Instance management
* Systems management

Figure 7   OMG Reference Model

The OMG Object Model defines a core set of requirements that must be supported in any system that complies with the Object Model standard. This set of required capabilities is called the Core Object Model and agreement was reached on these capabilities in 1992.

OMG Approach—Consensus, Fit for Purpose and Availability

The OMG's approach to standards is embodied in just a few words—consensus; fit for purpose; available.

OMG has created a forum where technical specifications can be arrived at through consensus. It has a formal process of issuing RFIs (Requests for Information) and RFPs (Requests for Proposal). These requests are issued by the Technical Committee. The Technical Committee supervises Sub Committees, Task Forces and Special Interest Groups (SIG). Sub Committees include those for Reference Model, Common Facilities and Object Model. Task Forces include those for Object Request Broker (CORBA), Common Facilities, and Object Services. SIGs include those for End-users, Portable Common Tools Environment (PCTE) and Business Object Management.

A landmark event for OMG and the development of object technology standards was the OMG's adoption of an Object Request Broker (ORB) standard in October 1991.

The ORB provides the mechanisms by which objects transparently make and receive requests and responses. In doing so, the ORB provides interoperability between applications on different machines in heterogeneous distributed environments and seamlessly interconnects multiple object systems.

1992 saw the availability of the published CORBA (Common Object Request Broker Architecture) specification (OMG and XOpen, 1992) and the adoption of CORBA Version 1 by over 50 computer manufacturers and software developers.

Public support for CORBA grew during 1993 to embrace over 80 companies. 13 Letters of Intent were received in December regarding technology submissions in RFPs, for CORBA 2.0.

The agreement of and availability of the CORBA 2.0 technical specification are likely to be determining events in the establishment of object technology. Objects created in a CORBA 1-based environment will not necessarily be able to interoperate with objects created in another CORBA 1-based environment. One of the key elements of the CORBA 2 technical specification is that interoperability of any and all CORBA 2.0 created objects is guaranteed. OMG believes that the consensus on object (software) interoperability is the only realistic goal within the domains of software development and software deployment.

Agreement of the CORBA 2.0 specification is expected by August 1994. In March 1994, CORBA 2.0 technology submissions were received by OMG from the following seven companies/groups of companies: OSF, Hewlett-Packard, DEC, NEC and Hyperdesk; SunSoft and Iona Technologies; IBM; Symbiotics; Expersoft; Bell Northern Research Europe; and ICL.

A major breakthrough is the definition of technical standards in Object Services was achieved in November, 1993 with the agreement on Volume 1 of OMG's Common Object Services Standard (COSS). This standard defines the three common services—naming, event notification and life cycle—on which most of the 17 other OMG identified Object Services depend.

OMG has many constructive close relationships with many standards bodies, industry groups and user groups. These relationships include those with The American National Standards Institute (ANSI), CFI, The Component Integration Laboratories (CI Lab), CIS, Corporation for Open Systems (COS), European Computer Manufacturers' Association (ECMA), ESPRIT, EUREKA, Institute of Electrical and Electronic Engineers (IEEE), IMA, International Telecommunication Union-Telecommunications Standardisation (ITU-TS, formerly CCITT), JIPS, National Institute for Standards and Technology (NIST), Network Management Forum (NMF), National Physical Laboratory (NPL), Open Software Foundation (OSF), Open Systems Interconnection/ International Standards Organisation (OSI/ISO), The Petrochemical Open Systems Consoritum (POSC), and X-Open.

OMG and Computer Aided Software Engineering (CASE)

Many of the leading CASE vendors are active members of OMG. These vendors include Amdahl, Andersen Consulting, Cadre Technologies, Interactive Development Environments, Intersolv, Kennedy Carter, KnowledgeWare, LBMS, Oracle, Softlab, Software AG and Texas Instruments.

OMG has strong links with the CASE community in general. These include the following:

- Liaision re. Concrete Object Model and OMG Object Model mapping.

- Liaison and interworking with Portable Common Tools.

- Environment (PCTE) standards groups. OMG is working with the

US Department of Defense and the US National Institute of Standards and Technology (NIST) to create a mapping of OMG's model which will be used to enhance the PCTE.

• Liaison with the Product Data Exchange Standard (PDES) groups.

• Liaison with groups involved with specifying Department of

• Defense Portable Common Interface Standard (PCIS) standard and the International Requirements and Design Criteria (IRAC) standard.

• Liaison with CASE Communique.

In early 1994, OMG formed a Special Interest Group (SIG) with the goal of fostering compliance with PCTE and OMG's OMA. This PCTE SIG is also charged with identifying requirements for, and fostering convergence of, interoperable CASE environments and fine grain repository tools for the evolution of PCTE.

In addition, the PCTE SIG hopes to work with users, vendors, academia and government, (as well as providing techical liaision staff to work with relevant consortia and accredited standards organisations) to assure consistent requirements for the evolution of PCTE to OMA compliance, object orientation and fine granularity standards.

PCTE was specified in standards prepared by Technical Committee TC33 of the European Computer Manufacturers Association (ECMA), and was adopted as a European CASE standard in 1991.

Analysis and Design Methods

There has been a plethora of object analysis and design methods developed and refined over the past four years. OMG made a major contribution to the market place in March 1994, by making available its *Object Analysis and Design, Description of Methods* (Hutt, 1994) report. This 200 page report describes, in some detail, 21 different object analysis and design methods in use throughout the world.

As most methodologies are in their infancy and are still being developed, OMG hopes this report will help developers in choosing a methodology.

Butler Bloor Ltd, a leading European IT strategy consultancy, recently stated (Howard and Foster, 1994) its belief that object oriented methods are destined to supersede existing methods, simply because they are more effective. However, Butler Bloor believes it will be a slow process.

CONCLUSION

Object technology experts and IT professionals, both in the US and the UK, are predicting a bright future for object technology. OMG is making progress in gathering the software industry together to agree one set of object technology standards, based upon existing technology.

The impact of object technology on CASE is currently being felt with the arrival of a host of new object oriented methods and the embodiment of object technology ideas. There is no clear consensus as to whether object technology will rejuvenate or replace existing CASE tools.

The biggest barriers to the speedy adoption of object technology seem to be organisational intransigence, incomplete standards and lack of suitably skilled object technology practitioners.

It is likely that the impact of object technology will be wide ranging, and not just limited to software development.

REFERENCES

Harries L and O'Callaghan A. *Object Technology in the UK, A Survey of Visitors to Object World UK 1993*. Object World Expositions, February 1994.

Howard P and Foster C. *CASE and Methods Based Development Tools, An Evaluation and Comparison*. Butler Bloor Ltd., 1994.

Hutt A T F. *Object Analysis and Design, Description of Methods*. Object Management Group/Wiley, 1994.

Jeffcoate J, Templeton A and Lachal L. *Object Technology: Suppliers, Products and Markets*. Ovum Ltd., in collaboration with Object Management Group, Inc., 1992.

Object Technology 1993-2001, Trends and Expectations, A Joint Study, OMG and Techvantage, July 1993.

Soley R M (ed.) *Object Management Architecture Guide, Revision 2.0*, OMG TC Document 92.11.1, September 1 1992.

Summary Findings: Survey of Attendees at Object World, Boston, January 1994. Object World Expositions (prepared by Marketing Perspectives, Inc.), 1994.

Summary Report,: Survey of Attendees at Object World, San Francisco, June 15-17 1993. Object World Expositions (prepared by Feedback Marketing Services Corp.), 1993.

Summary Report: Survey of Attendees at Object World, Boston, February 1-4 1993. The Object Management Group (OMG) (prepared by Feedback Marketing Services Corp.), 1993.

The Common Object Request Broker: Architecture and Specification, Revision 1.1. OMG Document Number 91.12.1, The Object Management Group and X-Open, 1992.

Section 4

Selected Software Tools

11

Software for Object Oriented Development

Leslie Jennison

The last chapter of this book contains overviews of software (and some hardware) demonstrated at the seminar. The development and use of some software is also described in the preceding papers. The intention is to provide enough information for you to decide if you are interested in evaluating or using any of these products, and to give you the UK and USA contact points so that you can obtain further details.

Details appear in product name sequence, and the information is as given at the time of going to press in April 1994. The editors would like to thank the staff of suppliers for supplying the information (sometimes at short notice). For each product there is a short description giving:

- The name of the originating organisation.

- The status of the product: whether it is commercially available, for proprietary use only, or a research tool.

- The year of introduction.

- An indication of the price: where possible giving the price per user,

Business Objects: Software Solutions. Edited by Kathy Spurr, Paul Layzell, Leslie Jennison and Neil Richards
© 1994 John Wiley & Sons Ltd

or assigning the price per user to one of the following bands—lower (less than £500 or $500), medium (around £2000 or $2000) or upper (£5–8000 or $5–8000) (some suppliers have chosen to provide prices on application).

- The name and address of the supplier in the United Kingdom, and in the USA.

- The key features as stated by the supplier.

- The supplier's brief description of any development methodology used or supported.

- Operating environments in which the software can be used for development and operation.

- Interfaces to other development tools.

- A short illustration, provided by the supplier, of how development is achieved.

The inclusion of products in this book is for informational purposes only, and constitutes neither an endorsement nor a recommendation of quality or fitness for purpose. The publisher and editors assume no responsibility with regard to the performance or use of these products.

This section is not intended to be a complete catalogue of products that can be used. In particular, we have not included products applied principally to writing object oriented code. The editors are happy to receive information about other tools for object oriented development.

ASCENT VERSION 3

Originator:

Octacon Ltd in association with Teesside University

Status:

Commercially available product

Year of introduction:

1994

Price details:

Less than £1000

Supplier in United Kingdom and in USA:

Octacon Ltd
102 Borough Road
Middlesbrough, TS1 2HJ
Tel: (+44) 642 210 087 Fax: (+44) 642 210 518

Key features:

- Full support of the Coad Yourdon Object oriented method including Gen-Spec, Whole-Part connections, etc.

- Object method produces enhanced code templates including routine initialisation code.

- Full support of the Yourdon structured method, including DFDs, ERDs and structure charts.

- Fully featured diagramming tool, with various automatic routing options to produce readable diagrams.

- Full data dictionary, easy to use dialogues allow the user to fill in the details behind the diagrams.

- Full consistency and correctness checking carried out in real time, no batch processing. This includes checking within a single diagram and across the whole model.

- Simple C/C++ code templates are generated from both methods.

- Ascent allows a two way link to development environments. Code can be generated, edited and then read back into Ascent through special editor links. These links also allow Ascent to control the IDE so code can easily be navigated from the model.

Methodology support:

Structured (Yourdon) or Object oriented (Coad Yourdon)

Operating environment:

Ascent runs under Windows 3.1 using a standard Multiple Document Interface allowing multiple diagrams to be open at once. Also incorporates a floating toolbar and a status bar.

Interfaces to other development tools:

Generates code for Borland C++ (version 4) or Microsoft Visual C++ (version 1.5) compilers

Using Ascent:

There is a big gap between an object model and code. Ascent bridges this gap. Once code has been generated from a model then the user is usually given very little support. Because it is code they have not written, they can not be expected instantly to be able to use it. Ascent overcomes this problem by keeping a link between the user's model and the code it generates.

Ascent controls an interactive development environment, for example Microsoft Visual C++, from the user's model. A user can click on a particular part of their model and be taken to that piece of code in the editor. For example a user can go from an object's service in the object model to the actual code for that service in the development environment. This link helps the user navigate his code easily and quickly from a model that he is already familiar with. A user can change a part of the model such as the definition of a service and Ascent can rebuild the appropriate piece of code. However this is not always the way users want to work, they may want to change the code in the actual editor. Ascent also supports this way of working by allowing any changes to code to be read back into the model to update it.

Figure 1 shows a screen shot of an object model and Figure 2 shows a dialogue box used to define the contents of such an object.

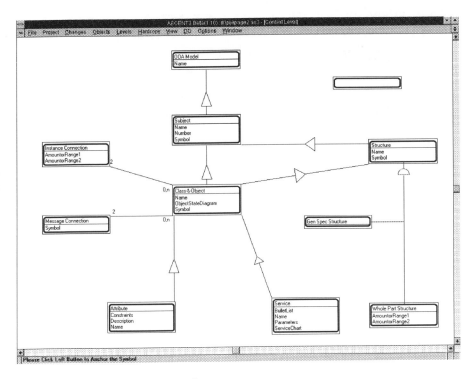

Figure 1 Object Model Screenshot

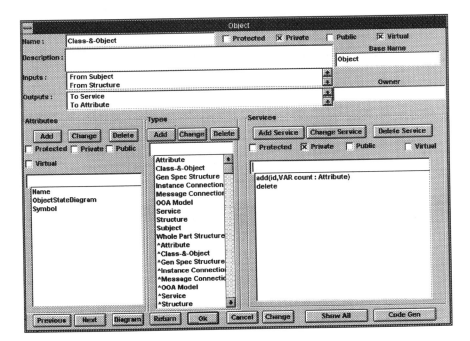

FUSIONCASE

Originator:

SoftCASE Consulting Ltd.

Status:

Commercially available product

Year of introduction:

1994

Price details:

Small Project Version £360
Single User Version £3000
Team Working Version £4000
C++/SmallTalk Toolsets £800

Supplier in United Kingdom:

SoftCASE Consulting Ltd.
The Loft, 13 Ravine Road, Canford Cliffs
Poole, Dorset BH13 7HS
Tel. (+44) 202 700415 Fax. (+44) 202 749643

Supplier in USA:

To be announced shortly

Key features:

Full support for the Fusion method
Online rule checking
Comprehensive QA reports
Automatic propagation of design decisions
Integrated search and query facility
C++ and SmallTalk code generation and reverse engineering facilities

Methodology support:

Fusion

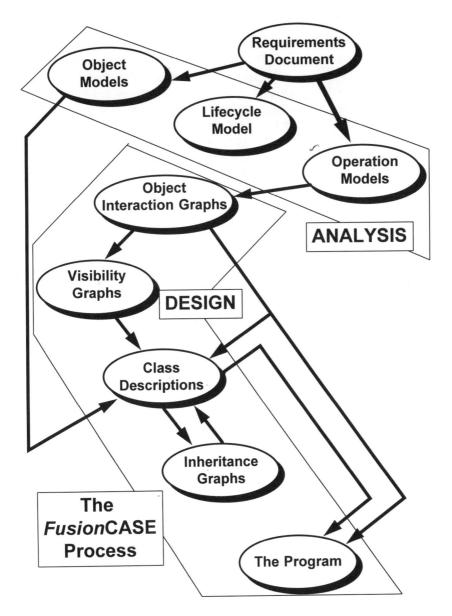

Figure 3   The *Fusion*CASE Process

Interfaces to other development tools:

SoftBench encapsulated—open interface + interoperability

Using FusionC*ASE:*

The Fusion method, originally developed by Hewlett Packard, claims to be the first second-generation Object oriented method. By building on the successful parts of earlier OO methods and addressing their weaknesses, Fusion provides a systematic route from a requirements document, through analysis and design, to implementation in programming language. *Fusion*CASE automates the support for Fusion increasing the level of achievable productivity (see Figure 3).

During analysis, a user develops models aimed at establishing the system boundary and the communication which flows between the system and its environment. During design, software structures are introduced to satisfy the abstract definitions produced during analysis. The design process explores the required operational characteristics by considering how objects interact at run-time, the implied visibility constraints and the exploitation of inheritance relationships. These results are documented in Class Descriptions which provide the foundation for implementation in a programming language.

The Language Toolsets integrate with the core product to provide seamless code generation and reverse engineering facilities.

A description of the thinking behind the development of *Fusion*CASE can be found in the Proceedings paper 'The *Fusion*CASE Experience', by Howard Ricketts.

INTELLIGENT OOA (I-OOA)

Originator:

Kennedy Carter Ltd.

Status:

Commercially Available Product

Year of introduction:

1993

Price details:

Price on application

UK Supplier:

Kennedy Carter Ltd.
1 Thornton Road
London SW19 4NB
Tel: (+44) 81 947 0553 Fax: (+44) 81 944 6536

US Supplier:

IPSYS Software
Suite 400, 338 Market Street
San Francisco, CA 94111
Tel: (+1) 415 693 9200 Fax: (+1) 415 296 2547

Key features:

- *Intelligent* OOA was designed to provide comprehensive support for a rigorous method (Shlaer-Mellor OOA/RD) and to provide completely non-redundant data entry for the analyst.

- *Intelligent* OOA was specified using the OOA/RD method itself, thus ensuring that the benefits of the method are flowed into the tool design.

- *Intelligent* OOA is designed around a central rule-driven database, rather than graphics editors supplemented by checkers. This intelligent pre-emptive checking ensures consistent and speedy construction of OOA models, even by novices. Analysts can enter information in any view (textual or various graphical) and I-OOA will update all other views automatically, generating diagrams if necessary.

Using an Action Specification Language (ASL), ANSI standard C code can be automatically generated from the analysis models. The generated code can either be used in the target system or in the host system debugging and simulation environment. This allows analysis model level debugging of the system (scheduled for June 1994).

- *Intelligent* OOA provides a number of integral features as standard such as:

  - Access control mechanisms including users and groups, and administrator roles.
  - Configuration management. Administrators can baseline and up-version domains and projects.
  - Project control. Administrators can lock and restrict access to domain and project versions for the purposes of reviews or testing.

Intelligent OOA is UNIX based and is available on a number of different hardware environments. It is provided with an application program interface permitting interaction with other third party tools, and has been designed for incremental development and adapted to meet the needs of specific clients.

Methodology support:

Intelligent OOA supports the Shlaer–Mellor Object oriented Analysis and Recursive Design (OOA/RD) system development method. The OOA/RD development life-cycle involves viewing the system as an assembly of distinct subject areas, or domains. Each domain is the subject of rigorous analysis using OOA, a detailed, precise and unambiguous analysis formalism. Because each domain is analysed as a separate subject area, concentrating on the services which it must provide without building in knowledge of the use to which the services are put, domains are highly reusable.

A special domain (the Software Architecture) addresses the issue of how the software is to be organised on the target system. Since OOA is so well defined, it is possible to define software architectures without regard to the actual analyses that have been produced using OOA. System designers can instead concentrate on the problems of control and data management in the target environment and the rules by which elements of an OOA analysis must be transformed into the system architecture. Such target architectures may be simple single tasks, or may be complex and distributed involving multiple tasks and processors. Like any other domain, software architectures may be reused in multiple systems. OOA/RD therefore readily lends itself to automatic transformations of analysis into code.

Operating environments:

Development environments are:

- Sun SPARC running SunOS 4.1.3 or Solaris 2.2 with OpenWindows or Motif.

- HP 9000/700 running HP/UX 9 with HP-VUE or Motif.

- IBM Risc System/6000 running AIX 3.2 with Motif.

I-OOA fully supports the X11R4 X Window System and so can be run on any of the above and can be accessed using X-Terminal software, such as X-Vision on a PC.

Intelligent OOA generates standard ASCII 'C'. This requires minimal system interfaces and can be ported to a wide variety of operating systems and real-time kernels.

Intelligent OOA also generates Progress 4GL.

Interfaces to other development tools:

- CDIF (CASE Data Interchange Format)

- Interface to ILOG KADS tool

- Interfaces to user defined products

Using Intelligent *OOA:*

Intelligent OOA allows analysts to develop models of system behaviours using the OOA/RD system development method. Domain models may be developed in any order and subsequently linked to projects, or projects may be defined first and domains chosen as a result. Within each domain the analyst is free to develop the domain model in any desired order.

The tool prevents inconsistent information being entered (but will never prevent the user from saving work), and prompts with existing information in all relevant places. Checks are provided for model completeness, and project managers may baseline and control access to versions of models for review or testing.

Automatic code generation can be used in conjunction with the provided host run time system to produce a simulation of the analysis models which can be debugged. This is achieved via a graphical user interface that behaves in an analogous way to source level debuggers.

Code generation can also be used with either the provided run time system or with a user developed run time system to generate the target application.

A fuller description of the development of *Intelligent* OOA can be found in the Proceedings paper 'Progress in CASE Support for Software Development Methods', by Allan Kennedy, Adrian King and Ian Wilkie.

OBJECTTEAM

Originator:

Cadre Technologies Ltd.

Status:

Commercially available product

Year of introduction:

1993

Price details:

Price on application

Supplier in United Kingdom:

Cadre Technologies Ltd.
Centennial Court, Easthampstead Road
Bracknell, Berks., RG12 1JA
Tel: (+44) 344 300003 Fax: (+44) 344 360079

Supplier in USA:

Cadre Technologies Inc.
222 Richmond Street
Providence, RI 02903
Tel: (+1) 351 5950 Fax: (+1) 351 6800

Key features:

ObjectTeam is a family of software development automation solutions
specifically aimed at object oriented development. The family consists of
two products: ObjectTeam for Rumbaugh, and ObjectTeam for Shlaer
Mellor. They provide support for:

- A comprehensive set of operating and database environments.

- Multi-user development with an active design object repository.

- The construction, assembly and reuse of software components and
  systems.

- Repository browser to view and edit every object and relationship stored in the object repository.

- Powerful script language can be directly modified by users.

- Object Model, State Model and Action Data Flow Diagrams.

- Domains and Subsystems.

Methodology support:

Rumbaugh *et al.* Object Modelling Technique
Shlaer Mellor OOA / Recursive Design

Operating environments:

- Development environments include: PC-Windows, Sun OS, Solaris, HP-UX, IBM AIX, Alpha OSF / 1, Silicon Graphics IRIX.

- Operating Environments are: 3GL languages—C, C++, Ada. 4GL environments are: Uniface, JAM, Visual C++, Visual Basic. Databases are: Oracle, Ingres, Sybase, Informix, ANSI SQL2, ONTOS, ObjectStore, Versant, Raima.

Interfaces to other development tools:

- Programming environments are: HP Softbench, IBM Workbench, SUN SparcWorks, Centerline ObjectCenter, Microsoft Visual C++, Uniface, JYACC Jam, Template Software SNAP

- Databases are: Oracle, Ingres, Sybase, Informix, ANSI SQL2, ONTOS, ObjectStore, Versant, Raima.

- Configuration Management tools are: Caseware CM, Atria Clear-Case, CMF, SQL Software PCMS

- Desktop publishing applications are: Interleaf, Framemaker, Microsoft Word.

ObjectTeam for Rumbaugh:

ObjectTeam for Rumbaugh provides complete automation for software construction using the Rumbaugh *et al.* Object Modeling Technique (OMT). Engineers can develop object oriented software designs that can be implemented in popular OO programming languages, and mapped onto object oriented and relational databases. The product provides full support for the feature rich notation afforded by the method, and is

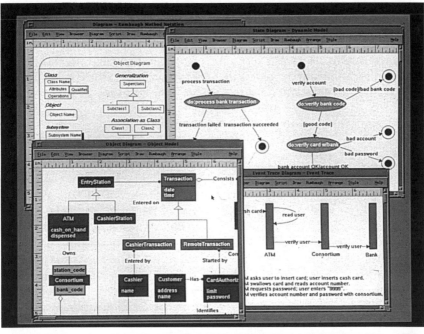

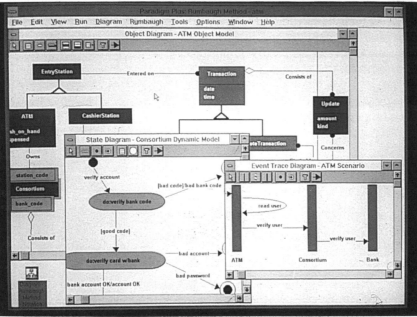

Figure 4 ObjectTeam

multi-user with an active design object repository.

ObjectTeam for Rumbaugh also supports construction, assembly and reuse of software components and systems, including links to programming environments and a repository browser to view and edit every object and relationship stored in the object repository. ObjectTeam's powerful script language can be directly modified by users. Scripts are provide for consistency and completeness checking, generation of comprehensive standard reports, code and database schema definitions.

ObjectTeam for Shlaer Mellor:

ObjectTeam for Shlaer Mellor fully supports the OOA 1991 method, published by Project technology. It provides support for all Shlaer Mellor work products and is able to derive many of the work products directly from data entered into the design object repository using the three basic views of Object Model, State Model and Action Data Flow Diagrams. OOA 1991 defines the concepts of Domains and Subsystems within an OOA context. Fully supported by ObjectTeam, these viewpoints make Shlaer-Mellor scalable onto the largest and most complex of projects, and domain mapping using Recursive Design enables automation of deliverable code from analysis models.

ObjectTeam provides comprehensive, multi-level checking which can be configured to suit the preferences of a particular project. ObjectTeam also provides support for the Shlaer–Mellor subsystem notebook for reports, or developers can generate reports to meet their own reporting requirements.

Cadre's experience of using OO development can be found in the Proceedings paper 'Managing the move to Object Oriented Development', by Nick Whitehead.

RATIONAL ROSE

Originator:

Rational

Status:

Commercially available product

Year of introduction:

1992

Price details:

Windows and OS/2 platforms start from £695
UNIX Platforms start from £1895

Supplier in United Kingdom:

Rational Technology Limited
Olivier House, 18 Marine Parade
Brighton, East Sussex BN2 1TL
Tel: (+44) 273 624814 Fax: (+44) 273 624364

Supplier in USA:

Rational
2800 San Tomas Expressway
Santa Clara, CA 95051-0951
Tel: (+1) 408 496 3600 Fax: (+1) 408 496 3636

Key features:

Rational Rose is a graphical software engineering tool that supports object oriented analysis, design and implementation, helping team's produce applications more effectively. Key features are:

- Support for the revised Booch notation that unifies object oriented analysis and design notation.

- Captures your analysis model.

- Supports model transformation from analysis and design.

- Represents your design model.

- Scales well from small to large projects.

- Solution available that automates the production of code.

- Preserves changes to code through each iteration.

- Facilities reuse of existing components via reverse engineering of code.

- Backed up by Rational's training and consulting services.

Methodology support:

Rational Rose supports the Booch 1993 notation developed by Grady Booch and Rational and published by Benjamin-Cummings in *Object Oriented Analysis and Design with Applications.*

Interfaces to other development tools:

Any C++ Compiler
Any Configuration Management system

Using Rational Rose:

Rational Rose supports object oriented development by automating the use of the Booch notation and by generating the application code from the design model. Rational Rose accelerates your transition to object technology by supporting the creative process of object oriented analysis, design and implementation.

The Booch method provides a complete set of constructs to communicate the results of your requirements analysis and your domain model. Using scenario modelling, the Rational Rose object diagram editor helps you capture your application's 'case of use'. During the domain-modelling phase, the class-diagram editor helps you represent the structural aspects of your application.

To transform this analysis model into a design model you refine the components (class, object, association, message passing) into more precise entities that you can describe from a design perspective. Each element of the system can be transformed be refining it or by changing its type. Rational Rose makes this process easy by providing the facilities to make incremental refinements to your domain analysis to produce a design architecture.

Rational Rose further assists the team during each step of the design process, from identifying the initial architecture, to the logical design, to the mapping to a physical architecture, to the final implementation in the programming language.

SELECT OMT PROFESSIONAL

Originator:

Select Software Tools Ltd

Status:

Commercially available product

Year of introduction:

1994

Price details:

£995 per user

Supplier in United Kingdom:

Select Software Tools Ltd.
High Street, Prestbury
Cheltenham, GL52 3AY
Tel: (+44) 242 226553 Fax: (+44) 242 251491

Supplier in USA:

Select Software Tools Ltd
Suite #84, Brookhollow Office Park
1526 Brookhollow Drive
Santa Ana, CA 92705
Tel: (+1) 714 957 6633, Fax: (+1) 714 957 6219

Key features:

Select OMT Professional provides support for the development of client-server systems using OO technology. Some key features are:

- Support for methodology life-cycle, architecture, techniques.
- Prototype generation in Visual Basic.
- High quality code generation in Visual Basic and Visual C++.
- Generation of client-server objects.
- Generation of relational tables from object models.

- Code regeneration.

- Support for enterprise modelling including merge facility and collision control.

- Open repository using OLE automation.

- Intuitive windows interface—CUA compliant.

- Powerful integrated dictionary.

- Context sensitive diagram editors.

- Completeness and consistency checking.

- Multi-user.

- Project administration.

- Comprehensive reporting and multi-page printing.

- File export facility.

Methodology support:

The development methodology supported by Select OMT Professional has the following characteristics:

- Business processes are used to drive the analysis and design process.

- A 4-Schema Architecture enables re-use of corporate objects and supports distributed systems.

- Object oriented techniques (drawn from Rumbaugh's Object Modeling Technique) are used to smooth and shorten the life-cycle.

- Incremental delivery is a key element of the life-cycle, as is iterative prototyping.

- Estimating is built into the life-cycle.

Operating environment:

Microsoft Windows

Interfaces to other development tools:

Microsoft Visual Basic and Visual C++, Borland Turbo C++. Select OMT Professional can be configured to interface with any Windows C++ compiler.

Using Select OMT Professional:

Select OMT Professional provides a development environment where the business modelling paradigm is designed to match the implementation paradigm. Techniques such as object modelling, prototyping, business process specification using object interaction diagrams, and dynamic modelling are used to develop the selected increment (based on business processes). Objects are identified in terms of 4-schema architecture layers. Visual Basic and Visual C++ code is generated from the specified increment, the close integration of Select OMT Professional with these products also facilitating iterative enhancement work. Relational schema can be generated from the model for RDBMS implementation.

A full description of the architecture, life-cycle and techniques supported by Select OMT Professional can be found in the Proceedings paper 'Developing Client-server Systems using OO Technology', by Stuart Frost.

SOFTWARE THROUGH PICTURES/
OBJECT MODELLING TECHNIQUE (STP/OMT)

Originator:

IDE (Interactive Development Environments) Inc.

Status:

Commercially available product

Year of introduction:

1993

Price details:

£5000 to £8000 per concurrent user seat

Supplier in United Kingdom:

IDE (Interactive Development Environments) UK Ltd..
1 Stirling House, Stirling Road,
The Surrey Research Park
Guildford, Surrey GU2 5RF
Tel: (+44) 483 579000 Fax: (+44) 483 31272

Supplier in USA:

IDE (Interactive Development Environments) Inc.
595 Market Street, 10th. Floor,
San Francisco, CA 94105
Tel: (+1) 415 543 0900 Fax: (+1) 415 543 0145

Key features:

- StP provides an integrated multi-user CASE environment for project support, across a range of UNIX workstation environments.

- Provides support of the full OMT notation, and development process.

- Navigation and full diagram and model checking is supported between all OMT models.

- Built on a powerful Core technology that provides common services to all products in the StP family, such as browsing and navigation, query and reporting, as well as generic diagram and table editors. Editors are configured via rules files, which dictate shapes, formats and methodology constraints. This provides a consistent look and feel across the editing environments in all StP products.

- User customisation is supported via the rules files, but the method constraints of OMT can not be violated.

- Open Data Dictionary and Repository architecture provides support for a range of user definable Query and Reporting activities.

- The StP central Repository is implemented via an Object Management System over a standard commercial RDBMS.

- Version control of models and diagrams via the host platform version control or 3rd. party Configuration Management tools.

- Powerful user definable abstraction filters can hide, show, select, flash, etc. symbols and details in complex diagrams to display and print a wide range of user viewpoints.

- The document management system allows detailed templates of text, annotations and diagrams to be stored, then run against a project repository providing a wide range of user, quality, management and user-specified deliverable reports to be published automatically.

Methodology support:

The Object Modelling Technique, OMT as proposed by James Rumbaugh *et al*.

Operating environment:

UNIX

Interfaces to other development tools:

The StP environment also provides links and integration to a wide range of 3rd. party tools and environments for Code Debug and development, DTP (Desk Top Publishing), Configuration Management, and Requirements Management, etc. for example DTP; Interleaf, Frame. RTM (Requirements Traceability and Management). CentreLine Software's CodeCentre and ObjectCentre. HP SoftBench environment, and many more.

Using Software through Pictures/Object Modelling Technique (StP/OMT):

IDE, in collaboration with the official mentors of OMT, the Advanced Concepts Centre (ACC) of Martin Marietta, have created a powerful UNIX implementation of OMT StP/OMT. StP/OMT provides life-cycle coverage from concept to OO code generation in various OO languages and Ada, for multiple user work groups and projects. Class capture of existing C++ code and libraries, with repository browsing facilities, makes access to and reuse of information very productive.

In addition, IDE provides a wide range of software engineering CASE (Computer Aided System Engineering) tools, for Yourdon related Real-Time Structures Analysis and Design, including Information Modelling in Chen or Bachman. The tool environment supports Requirements analysis to code implementation in a variety of languages, including C, C++, Ada, ANSI SQL, etc.

The StP (Software through Pictures) product Family includes:

- StP/OMT OMT (Object Modelling Technique).

- OO Analysis and Design, including C++.

- StP/SE Structured Environment: Yourdon related Real-Time Structures Analysis and Design, RTSA/SD.

- StP/IM Information Modelling in Chen or Bachman—Entity Relationship Analysis.

- StP/ADE Ada development, including forward and reverse engineering.

- StP/CDE C development, including forward and reverse engineering.

- StP/TestMaker 'T4' Test Case generation, integrated with the above environments.

More about OMT can be found in the Proceedings paper 'OMT Development Process, Vintage 1994', by Don Kavanagh.

SYSTEM ARCHITECT

Originator:

Popkin Software and Systems Inc.

Status:

Commercially available product

Year of introduction:

UK—1989

Price details:

From £1350

Supplier in United Kingdom:

Real Techniques and Methods Ltd.
118-120 Warwick St.
Royal Leamington Spa, Warwickshire, CV32 4QY
Tel: (+44) 926 450858 Fax: (+44) 926 422165

Supplier in USA:

Popkin Software and Systems Inc.
11 Park Place
New York, NY 10007-2801
Tel: (+1) 212 571 3434 Fax: (+1) 212 571 3436

Key features:

- Easy to use.
- Multi method—integrates OO and structured analysis and design (Information Engineering, SSADM) within a single encyclopaedia.
- Multi user support with diagram and record locking, and data dictionary or encyclopaedia merging.
- Provides requirements tracking through the entire OO life cycle
- Users can define additional metadata attributes and edit rules.
- Allows automatic creation of GUI windows from classes.

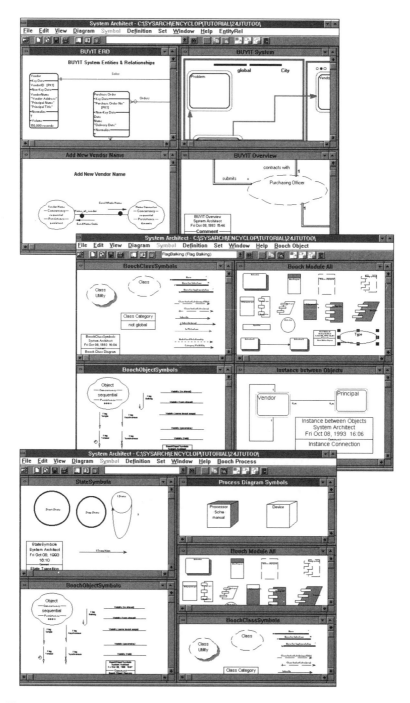

Figure 5 System Architect Windows and Symbols used to Define a System Structure, Object Classes and Objects

- Project Documentation Facility supports report production.

- Interfaces to client-server development tools.

Operating environments:

Windows 3.1
Windows NT
OS/2

Methodology support:

Booch, Coad
Yourdon
Shlaer/Mellor
Rumbaugh/OMT to be implemented by July 1994

Interfaces to other development tools:

Interfaces are available to a range of third party tools including most commonly used CASE tools, spreadsheets, and Windows development tools (for example PowerBuilder, Gupta Team Windows, Uniface, Visual Basic).

Using System Architect:

The screen snaps in Figure 5 show a selection of the windows and symbols used to define a system structure, object classes and objects.

TEXEL

Originators:

TEXEL Tool—Virtual Software Factory Limited
TEXEL Method—Putnam P. Texel

Status:

Commercially available product

Year of introduction:

1992

Price details:

Prices on application

Supplier in United Kingdom:

Virtual Software Factory Limited
Crest House, Embankment Way
Ringwood, Hants. BH24 1EU
Tel: (+44) 425 474484 Fax: (+44) 425 474233

Supplier in USA:

None

Key features:

- Closely supports the Texel OO method with use-case based requirements capture, candidate object class identification and disposition, static and dynamic modelling, design modelling and code generation.

- Supports consistency and completeness throughout the development process.

- Provides comprehensive context sensitive help.

- Constructed using the VSF meta-case tool. This, plus semantic code gives Texel unrivalled ability to incorporate new diagram types, report types, and links to other toolsets.

Operating environments:

- SUN Sparcstation: MOTIF

- IBM PS/2-OS/2: PM, IBM RS/6000 (RISC)—AIX: MOTIF

- DECstation—Ultrix: MOTIF, VAXstation—VMS: DECwindows

- IBM PC: Windows 3 (available 1994)

Interfaces to other development tools:

Currently Texel-SF is linked to POET OODBMS and IPL's Cantata and Ada Test testing tools. Any other tool interface can be provided on request.

TEXEL is also linked to software application re-engineering toolsets from VSF Ltd. There are plans to link the methodology and the Texel-SF workbench to RTM and a Repository of Reusable Components, at both the Object Class and Instance levels.

Methodology support:

The Texel Method (Texel 1993) is an amalgamation of features from other principle OO methods, driven by clients' requests from both the scientific and MIS community. The method has been successfully employed in both the scientific and MIS communities, in the USA and in the UK. Its success is based on a pragmatic approach to transitioning an organisation to the successful incorporation of Object oriented Technology.

The method is a blend of event and data driven philosophies that attempts to provide the best of both approaches to the community, while the tool provides a simplified user interface above a rigorous definition and collection of Object Classes. This combination offers the potential for an organisation to increase its Software Engineering Institute (SEI) Capability Maturity Model (CMM) level to a level 2 at least, if not to level 3. The Activities and Processes are well defined and articulated both graphically and textually.

Requirements Engineering
This first major activity uses Jacobson's Use Case model (Jacobson *et al.,* 1993) for Requirements generation and trace. Both static and dynamic Requirements Trace are supported by the VSF Texel tool. Use Cases are traced to the Subsystems that participate in the implementation of the Use Case, to the Object Classes within the Subsystems, and to the Methods within the Object Class. That relationship is kept both as a static view, and as a dynamic view which supports sequencing.

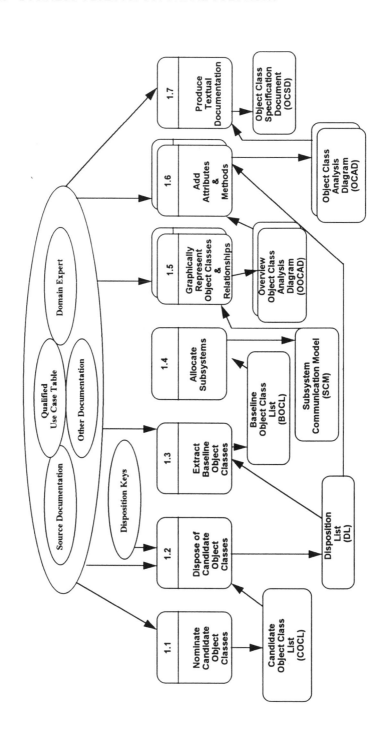

Figure 6   Object Oriented Analysis Static View

Object Oriented Analysis (OOA)

Figure 6 presents the Static View Activity. The Texel method uniquely provides a formal Candidate Object Class List (COCL) that is refined using pre-defined Disposition Keys, to a Baseline Object Class List (BOCL). The Baseline Object Class List becomes the basis for Subsystem identification. The formal Candidate Object Class List (COCL) provides an 'open' system to link quickly and efficiently with other front ends for example IDEF, or any other process description method/tool.

The Roles, Subjects and Qualifiers from the Use Cases are automatically entered into the COCL and disposed of as Object Classes—ensuring their consideration for Subsystem selection, but more importantly providing an earlier identification of Subsystems.

Shlaer/Mellor Information Structure Diagrams (Shlaer, 1988) (renamed Object Class Analysis Diagrams) form the heart of the static view of OOA. One major change from the Shlaer–Mellor method is the addition of List Attributes, which are permitted and encouraged (specifically within MIS systems). Aggregation and multi-level views further strengthen the Shlaer/Mellor concept. OMT notation further clarifies the static view (Rumbaugh *et al.*, 1991). The Object Class Specification Document (Shlaer, 1988) has been expanded by the addition of methods identification and Methods Descriptions, Ancestor/Descendant and Composite/Part descriptions—all of which are then captured by the Texel tool and automatically contribute to the draft of the graphical representation of the OOA solution and accompanying PDL.

The dynamic view shown in Figure 7 represents an enhancement to the traditional state model (Shlaer, 1992) by applying Use Cases as External Events and the addition of sub-states, as in PTech (Martin, 1993), to support re-use across application domains. Jacobson's interaction Diagram(ID) begins to form a bridge between OOA and OOD. This bridge appears to be particularly useful within the MIS community because the application domain is less 'concrete', and State Models can be categorised resulting in Object Classes having similar State Models. Many Object Classes have trivial, and perhaps no, applicable State Model at all—permitting a more efficient transition to the design activity.

Object Oriented Design

Object Oriented Design (OOD) (Booch, 1993) describes (graphically as well as textually) the overall Software System Architecture. The graphic representation is based on symbology initially created by GTE for a representation in Ada and expanded/refined by Texel & Company, Inc. to be a language independent OOD representation of the resulting software architecture.

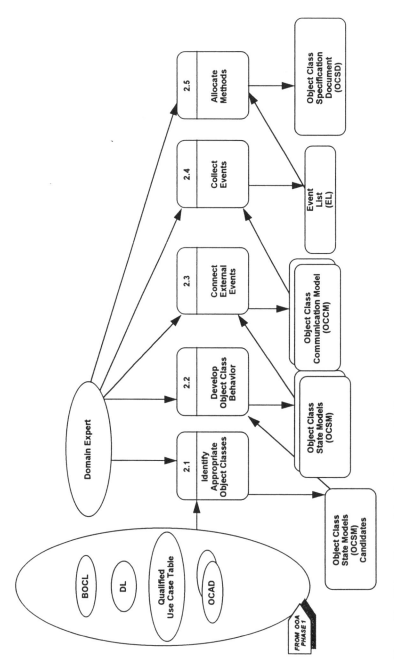

Figure 7 Object Oriented Analysis Dynamic View

The textual representation, or language specific Program Design Language (PDL), is dropped automatically from the tool in either Ada 83, Ada 9X, or C++. Using a language as its own PDL in this way allows early identification of design errors, and early initiation of interface testing. This is due to the compilation of files to verify visibility between Object Classes and ensure calling conventions are adhered to between Object Classes

Language specific Object Class declarations and implementation (structure only) are dropped by the tool Texel-SF, and are customisable with respect to file templates, database integration and test tool selection to form the beginning of a complete integrated development environment.

References:

Booch G. *Object Oriented Design with Applications.* Benjamin Cummings, CA, 1993.

Jacobson I, Christenson M and Jonsøn P. *Object Oriented Software Engineering: A Use Case Approach.* Addison-Wesley, MA, 1993.

Martin J. The Principals of Object Oriented Analysis & Design. Prentice Hall, NJ, 1993.

Rumbaugh J, Blaha M, Premerlani W, *et al.*[*Object Oriented Modelling & Design.* Prentice Hall, NJ, 1991.

Shlaer S and Mellor S. *Object Oriented System Analysis: Modelling the Real World in Data.* Prentice Hall, NJ, 1988.

Shlaer S and Mellor S. *Object Life Cycles: Modelling the Real World in States.* Prentice Hall, NJ, 1992

Texel P. *The Texel method: A Pragmatic and Field Proven Approach to Object Oriented Software development.* Available from Texel & Company, Inc. and from VSF Ltd., 1993.

VISUALAGE

Originator:

IBM Corporation

Status:

Commercially available product

Year of introduction:

1994

Price details:

VisualAge £1372
VisualAge Team £2473
VisualAge COBOL Component £823
VisualAge Multi-Database Component £549
VisualAge Communications/Transaction Component £963
VisualAge Multimedia Component £274

Supplier in United Kingdom:

IBM United Kingdom Ltd.
Tel: (+44) 705-492049 Fax: (+44) 705-214705

Supplier in USA:

IBM USA
Tel: (+1) 1-800-IBM-CARY Fax: (+1) 919-469-7423

Key features:

VisualAge is an integrated, application development environment designed especially for client-server, mission-critical, line of business applications through visual programming and construction-from-components technologies. It provides a series of high productivity, OS/2 based power tools for the development of applications targeting OS/2 execution systems. IBM plans to make VisualAge for Windows and VisualAge System Object Model (SOM) support for OS/2 available during 1994.

There are two base products in the VisualAge family: 'VisualAge' for the individual user, and 'VisualAge Team' for team development, which provides all the functionality of VisualAge plus support for team programming.

Using popular relational databases, VisualAge enables users to develop client-server database applications. In a server-based development environment it can produce complete on-line transaction processing (OLTP) client-server applications for OS/2. The user can build workstation applications that access remote transaction programs through a variety of network protocols and access data in remote and local relational databases.

VisualAge provides the following functionality:

- Visual programming (construction-from-components) which enables the development of complete applications from pre-existing or custom-built components with little or no knowledge of the underlying language.

- Support for team programming enabling multi-users complete access to the development environment and suite of productivity tools.

- Library services including versioning and release control that provide complete library code management so that large complex development efforts can be successful.

- Support for reusing programs developed in C, COBOL or any language which creates DLLs. This capability promotes the reuse of existing code, reducing development cycle time and future maintenance requirements. C support is included in the base VisualAge and VisualAge Team products. COBOL support may be ordered separately.

- Advanced graphical user interface (GUI) capability, including support to implement CUA '91 user interface controls.

- Communications and transaction processing components which provides a diverse menu of protocols with a simplified common access, including TCP/IP, APPC, and CICS OS/2 External Call Interface.

- Database components for interfacing with both IBM and non-IBM databases which provides a menu of databases with a simplified common access, including DB2/2, Oracle, Microsoft SQL Server. DB2/2 support is provided in the base VisualAge and VisualAge Team products. The additional database support may be ordered separately.

- Visual SQL query builder capability.

- Multimedia capability which provides a library of pre-defined, reusable and extensible components enabling the combination of audio and video into large, interactive, line-of-business applications. Multimedia can also be integrated into existing applications.

- Performance tuning and packaging tools.

- A complete application development environment which integrates SmallTalk editors, browsers, debuggers, inspectors, performance profiler and Dynamic Link Library builder.

Operating environment:

OS/2 (Windows support planned during 1994)

Interfaces to other tools:

- SOM/DSOM, Class Libraries

- DDCS/2, DB/2, DB2/2, Oracle

- Envy Developer, Microfocus COBOL, CICS OS/2

Access to other applications such as IMS Client/server/2, allows the development of applications for open distributed environments. VisualAge's open architecture enables the developers of GUI tools, database and communications support products and class libraries to write to published APIs.

IBM plans to address additional development environments and expand its communications and database access capabilities.

An Overview of VisualAge

VisualAge is an application development environment and suite of power tools which introduce technologies that unlock the complexities of application development in a client-server environment. Within its object oriented development environment, VisualAge provides visual programming. This technology enables the developer to work with the end user in an iterative manner to develop the client portion of client-server applications with very complex GUIs and accurately capture changing user requirements.

VisualAge provides many opportunities for reusing proven designs and stable code. VisualAge was developed using VisualAge itself; this assures that the design and code supplied with VisualAge have been tested and optimised. The ability to reuse existing code reduces development cycle time and, because many of the components can be reused without change, drastically reduces errors.

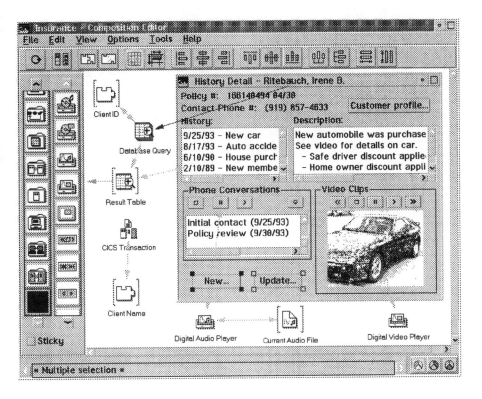

Figure 8   VisualAge Application Development Environment

Object oriented technology is emerging as the most promising avenue to solve the right sizing and client-server challenges of the future. VisualAge utilises this technology to simplify the development of applications for OS/2 in a graphical environment using construction from components. Additionally, more experienced developers have the benefit of the underlying SmallTalk language including an integrated suite of productivity tools (editors, browsers, debuggers, inspectors). These two approaches enable developers of various skill and experience levels to create mission critical client-server applications.

CASE

on Trial

Edited by
Kathy Spurr
Analysis Design Consultants
Chairman, BCS CASE Specialist Group

and

Paul Layzell
Department of Computation, UMIST, Manchester, UK

CASE has featured prominently in the computer press and sales literature, but is there hard evidence that any of the various claims made about it are justified?

This volume presents some actual user experiences, some comparisons and surveys, and some discussion about how the technology might be developed.

Those who have either invested already in CASE or are thinking of doing so in the near future will find some useful pointers here to the sort of questions which need to be addressed.

The material will be of interest to managers of Data Processing/Information Systems functions; all levels of systems development staff; Data Managers; Business Analysts and Consultants; those in the academic world seeing current CASE experience from other academics or practitioners; and interested User Managers and Information Systems strategists.

Kathy Spurr is Director of 'Analysis Design Consultants', which provides specialist consultancy and training in methods and tools for CASE. Previously, she was Principal Lecturer in Computing at the Polytechnic of North London. She is Chairman of the British Computer Society CASE specialist group.

Paul Layzell is currently Senior Lecturer in Computation at UMIST and a Fellow of the British Computer Society. His teaching and research focuses on methods, techniques and tools to support the initial stages of software development: fact capture, requirements analysis and specification. He has worked on several Esprit and Alvey projects in the methods and tools area and has provided consultancy and training on contemporary tools.

260pp   1990

ISBN 0 471 92893-3